# ROLE ~~MODEL~~ MOTHER

*One Mom's Journey to Parenting*

By

Telah Brown

# DEDICATIONS

This book would not be possible without the various individuals that God allowed to join me on this Parenting Journey. First, I want to thank my son, Micah Brown, for the unwavering support and encouragement as I completed this undertaking of completing this book. Next, my mom, who provided me a foundation of what I should and should not do as a mother when it came to being a parent and a role model. Then, I want to thank my siblings for accepting me for whom I am and encouraging me to follow my passion. Also, I want to thank my family and friends for the support and motivation as I completed this book.

Aside from the above mentioned, there were many men and women who played a significant role in Micah and my life over the years. To begin, I want to thank Micah's mentors, surrogate uncles, and friends who accepted him for him. To all the Role Mothers who provided a platform for me to express my frustrations, disappointments, and excitement as a mother without judgment. Words could never express how much each of you meant to my son and me over the years. I want to thank EB for all your tireless hours of working with me as I completed this book.

Ultimately, I dedicate this book to my son, Micah Brown, my niece, Labessie Monger, and my nephew, Donte Paskel! Additionally, this book is dedicated to all the Role Mothers and mentors in the world making a positive impact in the lives of children. Lastly, I want to thank God for trusting me enough in being Micah's mother.

# Foreword

Instantly, I was drawn to Telah Brown because of her infectious energy that seems to just leap off of her and onto anyone who is around her. That smile, her wisdom, and her out of the box perspective on life were just the icing on the cake as we developed a bond that still amazes me every day. As the mother of a son who is diagnosed with Attention Deficit Hyperactivity Disorder (ADHD), I wish there was someone like Telah around when I was fighting for his rights to be educated just like all the other children.

Unlike most parents, I had worked in special education, so I knew the policies and procedures related to accommodations for students with disabilities. Due to his disability, it required me to advocate for his rights as a student. When Telah and I discovered that we shared this commonality, my heart leaped with joy because it is rare to find a person who understands your struggles, but also your hopes and expectations for your child regardless to what label society tries to give them.

It is because of professionals like Telah that all children, especially children with special needs can live a full life without restrictions! Telah is one of the few who is willing to show you how to advocate for your child, how to push for modifications instead of placement in special education and how to create opportunities for your child to live a person-centered life. She is that breath of fresh air that so many parents have hoped for like I did so many years ago.

My son graduated from high school without ever stepping one foot inside of a special education classroom; I cannot say that our journey was easy or that it is over. As a college student, the challenges for my son has become even greater. Now it is him advocating for himself and using all of the techniques that were successful in helping him to graduate high school.

Having a child with special needs is not the end of the world, but sometimes, especially during the onset of diagnosis, a parent may feel that it is. In this book, Telah will show you how to navigate the educational system; how to create opportunities for growth for your child; how to develop a much needed village; how to remain sane when you want to pull all of your hair out; and how to love when it feels like no one loves you or your child back. Every child deserves a chance to learn, but that chance starts with you, their mother.

Dr. Carey Yazeed

# Table of Content

# The Mold of a Mother

Do you remember the exact moment that you were going to be a mother? Better yet, do you remember the exact age you were when you said, "I want to be a mommy!"? A lot of women can say that they knew they were carrying a child without it having to be confirmed by a doctor. Some women can also say that they remember what age they were when they committed themselves to *Mommy Hood*. But...All women can say that they did not control the timing, environment, or the way they became a mother. You as a mother had no control. Just as the mothers before you didn't have any control. We grow up dictating the plans that we want to put into place, but nine times out of ten our plans are overshadowed by destiny and life.

As a little girl, growing up, I wanted to have a lot of kids. It was all I knew. I had brothers and a sister. The commonalities between us were that we lived in the same house and did not have the same father. My mother died when I was only two weeks old. My mother's sister was the person that raised me. She is the only "mother" that I know. Despite my upbringing, I always wanted to have more than one child.

Although I grew up as a tomboy, who loved everything about sports, I fantasized about how I would raise my children. I quickly set boundaries as to how I was not going to raise my children – based on the things that I experienced growing up. I was subjected to alcoholism and domestic violence on a regular basis. Education was not a top priority within my family either. Those three relationship killers, alone, were my encouragement to want to do better when I had my own children. I wanted to give my children the best that the world could offer them. I wanted my children to grow up believing that they can become anything they set their heart and mind to.

I was determined to rise above the norm of most of those that I interacted with daily. I was gifted in basketball. So much to say, basketball was my ticket to college and to a life that I never knew. I knew at an early age that I wanted to help people, but my upbringing wasn't so welcoming to the advancement of a college education – mainly from a financial standpoint. Once I was accepted to college on a basketball scholarship, I put a plan into place that I knew I wouldn't fail to execute. Everything almost happened the way that I wanted it to. I encountered an injury while playing basketball that literally ended my collegiate career. During my healing process, I pledged for a well-known Sorority, and my eyes were opened to a different world. So much to say, that if I never experienced that injury, I wouldn't be writing this book today. There were some life lessons to be learned, but for the most part, I knew that my life was blessed.

I was picky about the relationships I entertained in college. I knew I wanted to be married, but I couldn't just marry anyone. I knew the person that I would eventually married would be the father of my children.  I took that into consideration in more ways than one.  I had a plan for my family that yet to exist.

# THE EARLY YEARS

## The Call of a Mother

So much for the plans that I had!  I was attending graduate school in Detroit, Michigan.  In my mid-twenties, and I still wasn't married nor did I have kids.  After multiple doctor visits, while attending graduate school, I was told that it would be difficult for me to conceive a child, let alone painful to carry one.  How is it that the anatomy of women unique enough to carry and bare children, but also the worse enemy to the women that have their hearts set on having children?

It was a time in life that I was very angry and resentful.  I was jealous of other women who were pregnant and about to give birth.  It felt as if my world had shattered.  I was utterly disappointed with God.  He made me a woman, and I couldn't have children!  That didn't make sense to me.  I thought of so many women who had the ability to conceive and have a child but choose to neglect their parenting responsibilities.  I questioned myself.  I vigorously questioned God.  I continuously asked Him, "Why give me this passion for children, yet I can never be a mother?!"  It felt as if my cries went unanswered for a period of time.  I wondered if my health would improve.  I wondered if there would be any possibility of me having children.  Only God knew what would happen in my life.

In my second year of graduate school, I had a professor by the name of Dr. Daniels. She always talked about her son. She loved her son dearly. The main thing that touched me about her, as a mother, was the fact that she loved her son – a boy that was born a different race. Yes, her son was adopted. I was intrigued with how a woman's love for a child that she did not give birth to was so powerful. She spoke of him as if she conceived him. She spoke of him as if she learned his temperament while he was in the womb. She spoke of him as if she remembered what his face looked like when he was born. But…Dr. Daniels didn't' experience any of it. She adopted a child that she loved instantly as if she gave birth to him. I wondered if I could ever experience a love for a child in the same way.

One night, after a long day, God spoke to me. He gently said, "Who said your child has to be conceived by you? If he is of Me, and I give him to you, then the child is your gift from Me!" Of course, I rolled over with the thought that I was imagining things and went to back to sleep. About a week later, a strong desire dropped in my heart to adopt a child upon graduation. I knew that Dr. Daniels' testimony and the word from God were not a coincidence. It was only a matter of me filling in the missing pieces.

Although I worked in the human services and education field for many years, I did not know the first thing about the adoption process. All I knew was that there were many children in the foster care system who needed a loving home. It always blew my mind to know that there were so many children that needed a home, but very few people that were willing to take them in. To know that, at times, I was angry at people and sad for the children that didn't choose to be born.

There was much that I needed to consider as I began the adoption process. I was single. I was in my mid-twenties. I was in an unfamiliar city without much family. I did have an older brother, Ertis, who was residing between two states. I was not married, let alone dating someone who was a potential to marry. I was not concerned about raising a child without a father, given my childhood. I believe that a child's parents should be more than involved and a part of their lives, but that is not always the case. I am living proof of that. I always wanted to have the *perfect* family, but when God authors your life, you can only trust that all will be well. I was in a place to open my heart and welcome a child that was not biologically mine. Just as my *mom* did for me. I knew I could not adopt a teenager, given my lifestyle and my age, but I knew that I could adopt a younger child. I just knew that regardless of who the child was, I would need to be prepared to deal with anything.

As graduation approached, I began to research various adoption agencies in the Detroit area. Two weeks before graduation, a classmate informed me of a credible adoption agency. I was somewhat apprehensive about contacting them, but I picked up the phone and dialed the number. By no coincidence, the agency representative informed me that there was an adoption informational meeting that evening. I eagerly RSVP'd for the meeting. It was like an outer body experience, as I hung up the phone. My road to becoming a mom was becoming a reality.

There were quite a few people at the meeting. The agency representative was very informative. I was full of excitement as I sat in the meeting room. I asked all the questions that were swimming in my head. I took all the notes that I could take. I gathered all information pamphlets that I could get my hands on. Things were moving forward. Things became more than hopeful.

As I evaluated becoming a mother and continued to conduct more research, I realized my one bedroom apartment was too small. I needed more living space to raise a child. I needed to find a place that could accommodate myself and a growing child. My brother, Ertis, lived in a large three-bedroom house. He didn't know my intentions on adopting a child, so I chose this as an opportunity to break the news to him. Ertis was ecstatic about me becoming a mother. His approval and kind words meant everything to me. "Telah, you will make a great mother!" are the words that I held in my heart as I continued to move forward on my journey to parenting.

Before I knew it, graduation day was upon me. I was set in my decision to adopt a child, and I planned to tell my family and friends on graduation day. After my graduation ceremony, I waited for the perfect time to tell my family and friends about my plans to adopt. As I spoke, my heart stopped. Raced. Stopped. I was anticipating everyone's response as I shared my news. Most were excited for me, especially my brother Drel, but some were also confused. Those that were confused wanted to know why I would want to raise a child that I did not birth. I explained my heart. I also explained that I have a supernatural love for a child that is not yet mine – that would eventually be mine and I would raise that child as if I was a "natural" mother. The confused group jumped on board, after hearing my heart, and said that they would support me in my new role as a mother.

Approval is one thing. Support is another. I knew I would need the support to be the best mother that I could be. Even before becoming a mother, I knew I would need the support physically, mentally, emotionally, and spiritually. I was ready for the unknown...But I knew the unknown would consist of me having a child to call my own. I didn't just want a child, I knew I wanted a son. A son that God named Micah.

## The Waiting Process

Some people say that adopting a child is equivalent to being pregnant and having a child.  You know that a child exists.  You know that this child will depend on you.  You just don't know when the child will be in your physical presence for you to love and raise.  Adoption, like pregnancy, is a waiting game.  Unlike a pregnancy, you do not have control of how or where the child is born.  You do not have control of the environment the child is introduced to, in the earlier days or months of his/her life.  Going through the adoption process, I knew I would have to be prepared to go through the ups and downs of the adoption process – knowing that I will ultimately end up with a child that I would nurture and love no matter what.

After graduation, I went into high gear with my research and inquiries about the adoption process.  I knew that I would have to partner up with an adoption agency to ensure that the adoption process went as smooth as possible.  About one week following graduation, I had an intake meeting with the initial agency that I visited for the information meeting.  I visited other agencies, but there was something that I connected with by visiting this agency.  They were awesome!  I decided to go through this agency to follow through with the adoption process.  I was assigned an adoption specialist by the name of Kim.  She was extremely knowledgeable and personable.  Between the paperwork and the preliminary interviews, I felt that it was a never-ending process. As part of the initial process, I was told that I would have to pass an in-home inspection. Once I knew that was the next step, I made the necessary steps to move into my brother's house. Ertis never hesitated when I called him. He assisted with the move and made sure that all loose ends were taken care of in the house to ensure that there weren't any red flags raised during the initial home assessment.

My friends were supportive with my new transition, as well. After my move, I had a paint party with those that were close to me. We painted. We decorated. It was as if I was really preparing for the birth of a son. My friends never made me feel as if I was out of place for not giving birth naturally. They made me feel as if I was a mother waiting to see her child for the first time.

The day finally came for the home visit. I was nervous, and I was excited! It was as if this was a surreal moment. I could not believe I was finally going through with this. Ertis was home for the assessment home visit. He wanted to show his support as much as possible. Kim arrived, and I knew there was no turning back. She toured the home and saw my son's bedroom that was recently decorated. That was the first of many inspection visits before I could even "identify" who my son would be.

The adoption process became a tedious and emotional process for me at times. I would receive reports on kids who were abandoned, born addicted to drugs and alcohol, and had experienced the worse in life that one could ever imagine in such a short amount of time. It was disheartening to know that I could not save every child whose profile crossed my path. I attended adoption fairs but did not like the manner in which the children were displayed. It baffled me as to how people would adopt a puppy in a heartbeat, but would not so easily consider adopting a child that is in need of a family. It seemed to me that the value of an animal's life is worth more than the life of a child. To me, that is more than an asinine concept. My heart ached as I silently wished this world was a better place. I began to turn down invitations from other adoption fairs because it just wasn't for me.

The adoption process changes you. It puts you in the mindset of wanting to be the best parent that you could be. You gain a better appreciation to be blessed and privileged to become a parent of a child that was born into a world of uncertainties.

## Could It Be?

There are specific moments that you remember as if it were yesterday because it changed your life that much. I remember the day that I received a phone call from Kim – telling me that there was a child that was adoptable. My first reaction was of disbelief. I guess because of the months that I previously experienced. There were many boys that were deemed adoptable, but things didn't seem to pan out. And having a moment of correction, I knew that God had a plan so this was ultimately going to work in my favor and in the favor of my son to be. I scheduled a time to meet with Kim to view the child's profile to see if this could really be my son.

As I read about this child, I could not believe what I was reading. This child experienced traumatic events before even being born. Following his birth, the doctors did not expect for him to survive very long. They had a list of reasons to validate their expectations. This child wasn't only abandoned by his mother, after birth, but he also had a health history that was not promising. This child did not receive any prenatal care when his birth mother was pregnant with him. He was exposed to drugs in the womb – being born addicted to crack cocaine and with the Respiratory Syncytial Virus (RSV). He weighed only one pound due to being born prematurely. Was in constant need of oxygen. Needed a heart monitor and was totally dependent on a breathing machine.

Ultimately, there was a potential that the child would end up blind. He was often referred to as the "Million Dollar Baby." This child's medical expenses literally cost the state of Michigan a million dollars to care for him. The state needed to exhaust many resources to keep this child alive. Due to this child's health issues, it was determined by his doctors that he would always be behind in all areas of growth, physical development, intellectual development, and socialization in comparison to other children his age. I began to cry for this child because he was only ten months, but in my heart, I knew he was "Micah" – the son that I was meant to have. Although I was sure in my heart that this would be my child, I still questioned how I could care for a child with so many medical challenges.

After reading and evaluating the profile with Kim, I agreed to meet "Micah" at his foster home the following day. Truth be told, this was the first and only child I decided to meet during the adoption process. Something within my heart knew that he was my son, even though my brain could not comprehend what was really going on. When I met "Micah," I fell in love with him immediately. The love I felt for him was indescribable. It was genuine. It was a love that I knew I didn't have to question. It was agape love at its purest form.

"Micah" was so precious, handsome, and small. Although he was only ten months, he was extremely busy and energetic! He was crawling and moving as if he knew no boundaries. This was a concern for me. I questioned myself and my abilities to handle a child with so much energy, but I knew God would not give me more than I could handle. I knew that the odds were against me with raising a child with such an intimidating health history. I knew that the love I immediately felt for "Micah" was the advocate of my internal peace for me to take on this role as a mother head on. I didn't have to think twice about moving forward with adopting this child that stole my heart. I told Kim to proceed with making the adoption legal. We sat down and talked about the next steps. She asked if I was sure about moving forward with the adoption process and I could only respond with "YES!"

As part of making the adoption legal, I needed to spend as much time as I could with my soon to be son. I had dinner with him and his foster family on many occasions. After a few nights with the family, Kim believed that it was time for me to start taking him out on for day visits. I had this day planned the moment I met this precious child. I wanted to be able to make his environment comfortable and fun. I introduced "Micah" to those that were closest to me. My friends loved him immediately. Ertis adored him like he like the son he never had. It was as if he was truly my own child and no one felt indifferent when they were around him. This child was a very happy child, and I wanted to do my best to keep him happy and to show him that he was loved.

The day visits eventually became overnight visits. The room that I prepared, before knowing who my son would be, became the safe haven that I prayed it would be. It was as if this was the child's home since the day he was born. Although I didn't have him full-time, we established a routine, and our bond became stronger. If a stranger were to visit us, they would've never known that he wasn't legally my child. It was the same in public. People couldn't tell that I wasn't his biological mother. It was an automatic assumption that we were tied together as mother and son. Some questioned if I had any reservations that something would go wrong during the adoption process – that wouldn't allow me to legally adopt "Micah." They saw how much time, energy, emotions, and love that I put into establishing a relationship with my son to be. My only response to those that questioned me was that I had enough faith that this was the son that God promised me. I could not believe any different because I knew it was true in my heart that he was my son and I could refer to him as such.

Time was flying by and before I knew it, "Micah" was turning a year old. I really wanted to make this day special for him. Because I was in the process of legally adopting my son, I was allowed to have a birthday party for him. In preparation for his party, I made it a point to buy him a birthday outfit and some new shoes. I took the child to a local Stride Rite to purchase him some white walking shoes. This was a true memory that I was able to store in the "Mommy's Book of Memories." There was a generous shoe salesman that was so helpful. He helped me measure the child's feet to ensure that I was purchasing the correct size. In a way, to me, the shoes were a symbol of moving forward, but boy was I in for a big surprise! The shoe salesman put the shoes on the child, and before I knew it, the child took off as quickly as possible, but he kept falling. I always thought that he couldn't walk. It was a sight to see! The shoe salesman then explained that the previous shoes that the child had on were too small for him. When shoes are too small for a child, that is learning to walk, that child is discouraged from walking by the pain that is caused by the shoes. That type of pain is too unbearable for such a small child. We immediately saw the relief on my son's face when he got the hang of walking in his brand-new shoes. This was a moment that I held dear and near to my heart. It was literally a moment of feeling as if I saw my son take his first footsteps – not making me feel as if I missed a major milestone in his life.

October 1, 1996, was another big milestone for me to add to my memory bank. It was the day that my soon to be son turned a year old. Who would've thought that such a small person, at such a young age, would capture my heart? I planned a big party to celebrate my son's birthday at Chucky Cheese. I invited family and friends. I wanted everyone to join me as I celebrated a life that meant the world to me. Despite the circumstances of "Micah's" birth, I was beyond thankful that I was able to be a part of his life at this given moment. He received so many gifts for his birthday. It was ridiculous! When the party ended, it took a while for Ertis and me to pack everything up. We had to split gifts between both of our cars since there were so many to carry home.

October was flying by as November was approaching. The adoption was not legalized yet, but I was still preparing for my life to change. My friends were supportive beyond words. Although I was not physically pregnant, my friends and co-workers still honored me as a mom to be. I was surprised with not just one baby shower…but with three baby showers. I knew that all who contributed to each baby shower not only loved me but also loved my son to be. I received so many gifts between all three baby showers. There were gifts of clothes, shoes, toys, and diapers. I also received a playpen, strollers, high chair, car seat, and crib. I received more than I ever expected or imagined. Because "Micah" was a preemie, he was small for his age, and the clothes would last a while as he grew into them.

There were plenty of overwhelming moments as I was being celebrated as a mom to be. I was overwhelmed by the love and support that those closest to me expressed. I just knew that there wouldn't be a moment that "Micah" would feel out of place or as if he didn't belong. He was being adopted into a family dynamic that was destined specifically for him. I couldn't wait, for the day, that he would legally become my son.

## His Name is Micah!

December 20, 1996, was a life changing moment that changed my world forever. I received a call from Kim. Her words left me in a state of shock, but also filled me with joy. Kim informed me that the foster family that was caring for "Micah" did not want him to return back to their home after Christmas. It was requested that he officially move in with me as soon as possible. I had "Micah" mostly every chance that I could get. He was only with the foster family for a short period of time, and I had him most of the time. The foster family was attached to "Micah," and it was becoming harder and harder for them to deal with things emotionally. Although I was overjoyed, by the news, I knew I needed to take their feelings into consideration. It wasn't as if the foster family were unfit. They loved "Micah" as much as I did. It was just becoming too much for them, knowing that the adoption process would soon end in my favor.

As I hung up the phone, I knew that I could officially call the child, that was a priority in my heart, by the name that was part of this promise. Micah. This was something that I couldn't have ever imaged as a Christmas gift. The symbolism of Christmas was not just a sign for me, it was prophetic in knowing that I now had the child that God promised to me. It was a humbling experience to know that God thought of me as being worthy enough to be the mother of a child born in the worse circumstances.

I shared the news with Ertis, and he was overwhelmed with joy too. He and Micah became inseparable, since the day they met. It was a bond that I knew would take place. It was part of God's promise that I did not have to worry about anything as I raised Micah as an unwedded mother. I knew that there would be many instances that my brothers, Ertis and Drel, would make it a point to show Micah how important he was to them. Not just as my son, but as a boy to a man.

There was so much to put into place, now that Micah was officially living with me. I wanted Micah to grow up with values, personal beliefs, and a support system that he could always depend on. I knew that I needed to appoint godparents to be a part of that support system. I prayed and asked for guidance about who those people should be. I knew that whoever was called to be Micah's god-parents would love him and support him just as much as I would. After much prayer, I knew that there were only two people, who were close to me, would be able to take on the role as Micah's godparents. For Micah's godmother, I chose Marcia - my friend and sorority sister. For Micah's god-father I chose Windale - my mentee and college student. Both were ecstatic and welcomed the role as Micah's godparents. They were very serious about their designated roles. Neither one of them will know how much I appreciated them both and their families for accepting Micah into their lives as they have.

One day, Micah and I were sitting around the house playing. It was a normal day for us until the Spirit of the Lord spoke to me. He said, "I will use Micah to touch millions." I asked God what He meant by that, and everything around me became silent. Even Micah got silent. He just sat there and didn't move – then turning his attention to what was on the TV. I sat in amazement for a few minutes. I had no idea what that meant. I immediately called Marcia and told her what just happened. She agreed that Micah would be called to do great things and hold notable positions in life. I also called Windale and told him what happened. He couldn't disagree with what was said. Both godparents were mature Christians, and it was moments like this that I needed their support. I knew from the day that God told me to adopt Micah, I would be raising a special child. But this new message from God upped the ante to let me know that despite how my child was born, Micah would be an influence on the world.

## **Growing Pains**

The weeks were passing by since Micah officially moved in with me. We established more of a routine…Until he started teething! This was something I never experienced before. Micah was not only teething, but he was also biting. Whoever was near him, he would grab them and bite them. It did not matter who they were or whether he knew them. He was a busy body and never sat still. It was hard to keep him under control and focused. And then I realized that a playpen is not just a gift that you give to a mother. A playpen is a life saver. If I were to tell you that Micah's playpen and I became great friends, that would be an understatement. Don't get me wrong. I did not put Micah in the playpen for any unnecessary reasons. As a single mother, I needed to tend to certain things for myself, and the playpen came in handy. When I needed to clean and cook, Micah was able to sit in the playpen as he watched television. It was what kept him safe and in an eye shot as I took care of day to day things. Micah eventually learned how to climb out of the playpen, but he was also smart enough to learn not to climb out of it unless I gave him the approval to do so.

As Micah got older, his health seemed to improve. He was a frequent visitor at the doctor. Between the issues with his vision and breathing, I needed to make sure that I stayed on top of everything so they wouldn't become more of a concern. Micah also had allergies that required medical attention, but I was able to manage it for the most part. It was easy to tell when Micah was really sick. He would sleep so much in one day, and sleeping was not Micah's typical behavior. When I knew that he was in a continuous sleep pattern, it meant that Micah was not feeling well. High fevers and rashes usually followed after the sleeping spells. The running joke in the hospital was that everyone knew when Micah was getting better because his energy levels became a challenge for the even the nurses to be able to handle.

Micah was such a wired child! I was no match for Micah as a twenty-something-year-old single parent. I had a wonderful group of friends who supported me and took turns assisting with Micah. As a single mother, I realized it took a village for me to be the best mother that I could be for Micah. Although it was my choice to parent him as a single mother, I knew that I needed help. I am a firm believer of accepting help when it is offered and asking for it when it is needed. If the person is genuine with their offer, I never turned away assistance when I needed it. I knew not to be prideful. I knew that the assistance would not only benefit me, but it would be an excellent experience for Micah as well.

Since recently becoming a parent, I was blind to rejection when it came to Micah. Everyone was accepting of Micah, despite his limitations and his abundance of energy. That was until I went to the one place that I would least expect to be rejected

– church.  Marcia and I agreed to go to church together.  As I arrived at the church's nursery, the leader of the youth department approached me hastily.  "Micah cannot attend class unless you are with him because he is all over the place!" Those were her words exactly.  I was in shock.  Marcia was in shock.  Her words caught me off guard.  Micah was attending class, regularly, before this and no one ever expressed a dissatisfaction with him being in class.  If this was brought to my attention before, I would've been able to assist the teachers with empowering them with the information they needed to know to keep Micah engaged while in class.  I felt ashamed, embarrassed and shunned.  How can someone, who is a leader in the church, act so unwelcoming and prejudice?  It wasn't as if I were one of those parents that just drops off her child and does not offer support to the ministry.  At any given moment, I volunteered to help out even when I wasn't scheduled to do so.  And now I was being told that Micah couldn't attend class unless I stayed in the class with him?  I was being rejected by the very place that was a place that I enjoyed being at and felt safe.  I wasn't the only being rejected, Micah was the main one being rejected.  I didn't want to be in a place where my child was considered a rejection.  Did I mention this was a church?  The very place that people should be able to go to and be at peace?  That was a joke!

I became angry with God.  I truly felt betrayed.  Again.  How could He allow this to happen?  The very place that exists, for His name sake, rejected my son and me! I began to feel that anyone was capable of rejecting my child if the church has rejected him. Then God spoke to me as He did in His signature way. He reminded me of a previous conversation. "I will use Micah to touch millions," He said again. I stepped back from my moment of anger and reflected on the promise. I eventually calmed down, but then I told Marcia that I will never allow anyone else to make me or Micah feel less than a person because of their choice to reject either one of us.

## 2 + 2 = 3 Kids Plus Me

In August of 1999, we relocated to Milwaukee, Wisconsin so I could be closer to my immediate family. My health was not great, and my family expressed that they wanted me to be closer to home – with a promise to help out. One year before moving back to Milwaukee, I gained legal custody of my nephew and niece. Now you may be asking, yourself, what in the world would possess me to take on two more kids. I can tell you. It pretty much made sense that I would be the best person to care for them. I also didn't want to see my niece and nephew live in the environment that I grew up in. Financially, I was good. I was focused on being a parent, and I wanted to make sure that my niece and nephew received a fair chance at life. I made room in my heart and my home to raise two more kids and give the best life as much as possible. At this point, I was a home owner with a large home and a great job as the Director of one of the largest domestic violence shelters in the United States.

I became a parent of three young children in a matter of two years. With two children (Micah and my nephew) having disabilities, I knew that I would need to be patient, implement structure, and maintain their medication and doctor visits on a regular basis. My nephew was six, and my niece was five when I became their legal guardian. My nephew, Donnie, was diagnosed with fetal alcohol syndrome, asthma, and attention deficit disorder (ADD). My nephew's behavior was deemed as extremely impulsive, which resulted in him being hospitalized on multiple instances. I remember, before we left Detroit, Donnie was hospitalized for two months. My niece, Bessie, was a girly girl. She liked to dress up, play with her toys and just be a little lady. Whenever one of my friends had a wedding, Bessie was the flower girl. She was so cute.

While transitioning to Milwaukee, I knew that I needed to find a job to offer some flexibility in my schedule so that I could be attentive to my children's need. God then blessed me with a position as a Program Evaluation Manager with the state of Wisconsin as well as an adjunct professor at the University of Wisconsin-Milwaukee. Next, I would have to find a school that catered to each child's individual needs, along with extracurricular activities that would stimulate their purpose and growth. I found a great school for Donnie, which was totally inclusive regardless of the students' disabilities. After some extensive research, I enrolled him in the school, and we both loved it! Donnie excelled academically and became a helper in the school. I provided a structured household for him outside of school, which included baseball, martial arts, and tutoring. On Saturdays, both he and Micah participated in martial arts which he did great at. For Micah, on the other hand, martial arts just was not his cup of tea.

Identifying a school for Micah was a bit more challenging. Mainly due to his age and lack of medical diagnosis. Although

Micah was going to the doctor on a regular basis, the doctors could not formally diagnose him with a specific disability. They just knew which medications would help Micah keep things under control. According to the doctors, Micah's young age played a factor. In Milwaukee, I identified an excellent doctor that was an expert in diagnosing rare disabilities in children. The doctor was accepting new patients, so I choose him as the children's pediatrician. It was a hopeful move because I truly wanted to be able to assist Micah and Donnie with their needs medically and emotionally.

As Micah went off to pre-kindergarten, he faced many challenges due to his vision and allergies. He was smaller than the other children that were his age, but his character and personality made up for it! All the students considered him their friend and the teachers adored him. Micah thought he was a big boy because he was going to school like his two cousins every day. It was rewarding, as his mother, to see him happy and having the typical four-year-old experiences. Micah admired Donnie and Bessie. They were all considered siblings – based on the bond that they formed. They shared everything. I believe having them in the household, at that time in Micah's life, worked for them and Micah.

If you recall, I moved to Milwaukee attached to a promise made by the family to assist me with the kids. Should I say that I knew in my gut that I was better off not leaving Detroit? In fact, my brother Ertis pleaded with me not to move to Milwaukee because my support system in Detroit was extraordinary. These are the very same family members that "nominated" me to become the legal guardians for Donnie and Bessie.

I had to find ways of managing all three kids and not becoming burnt out. Between juggling school schedules, after school activities, and my professional and personal life, you would think that I was competing for a Guinness Book World Record that never existed. All I truly had was the encouragement of others that I knew – from a distance. It was a true test of my faith in God as a mother and a person.

# I Want to Be a Star!

Micah struggled in school a great deal. He was struggling due to demands of school. Micah was struggling because of his hyperactivity, limited vision, allergies, and asthma. He was so brilliant that, at times, he thought he was the teacher during class. He always helped his classmates with the answers to the assignments, but this kid never did his own work. I got constant calls from his school about his behavior. You would think I was running a hotline as a side job. One day, I got ten calls. Yes! I received ten calls in one day about Micah running back and forth to the pencil sharpener. Believe that every problem called for a solution. The solution to Micah's pencil debacle was mechanical pencils. Micah was the only five-year old that I know to use mechanical pencils as a requirement.

After a while, Micah's doctor was finally able to provide a diagnosis for Micah. Micah was diagnosed with attention deficit hyperactivity disorder (ADHD) and severe asthma. Even though a diagnosis was provided, Micah still had to find ways to manage his day to day behaviors. One day, Micah told me that he was tired of always getting into trouble at school. He was so devastated that he cried himself to sleep. After researching a variety of medications, and in speaking with his doctor, I elected to start off with a highly-recommended medication to help him with his hyperactivity and impulsivity. Although I conducted a lot of research, I was concerned about the side effects of the medications and the effects it would have on Micah. Yes, he was becoming healthier each day, but I still had to take into consideration that he was born addicted to crack cocaine and his body weight was still considered to be below average. Micah's doctor did all that he could to reassure me that I was making the best decisions on behalf of Micah's medical needs. I knew there was much to consider, especially since this was a period of finding out what worked best for Micah.

I wanted Micah to be happy. I also wanted him to become more involved with certain things when needing to make certain decisions about his medication. Micah's doctor and I always made it a point to talk to him about the medication that he was taking. At the time, Micah was only five years old. He didn't understand much, but he was able to equate the medication as part of the solution for him to stop getting in trouble. The doctor explained to Micah that ultimately the results of his behavior is up to him. He also explained to Micah that there is no magic pill and that he needed to want to do better for himself. I liked this doctor for this very reason. He never used medication as the fixer-upper. He only prescribed medication as a way to manage the diagnosis, while encouraging Micah to still make the right choices. We tried a variety of medications until we found the right combination for Micah. Eventually, his hyperactivity minimized at school.

Micah could manage his day to day life for the most part. By the time he was six years old, Micah had developed into an amazing young boy. He was advancing in school. He exceeded expectations and being the kid that I prayed for him to be able to be. One-day Micah was sitting in the family room watching the *Cosby Show*. He came running into the kitchen yelling, "I want to do what Bill Cosby do!" Of course, I'm thinking to be a doctor because Bill Cosby was a doctor on the show. Not only that, Micah was fond of his doctor. Automatically, I thought Micah wanted to be a person that helps other people in the medical field. Micah yelled, "No, Mom! I want to be on TV like Bill Cosby!" I was shocked that Micah knew that he would want to be on TV at such a young age. But I was also asking myself, how in the world would I be able to get this boy to follow directions on the set of a television show, let alone follow directions at school?

# REFLECTION MOMENTS

1.  What were your dreams of being a mother when you were a child?

_____

_____

_____

_____

_____

2.  Why did you become a mother?

_____

_____

_____

_____

_____

3.  What fears do you face as a mother?

_____

_____

_____

4. What unique characteristic does your child(ren) have?

_____

_____

_____

_____

5. What areas do you find yourself needing the greatest support as a parent?

_____

_____

_____

_____

6. Who do you consider your support system?

_____

_____

_____

_____

7.  **What has your child expressed to you that he/she wants to do in life? (It is not your role to determine if their interests are realistic or not.)**

_____

_____

_____

_____

8.  **What programs/professionals do you wish existed to assist you as a mother?**

_____

_____

_____

_____

# <u>NOTES</u>

# ELEMENTARY YEARS

## What Is a Mother to Do?

For whatever reason, as Micah aged, his behaviors of hyperactivity seemed to worsen and so did his asthma. His hyperactivity and asthma dictated a lot of what he was able to do as a kid. Due to his high-energy level, I had to find activities that allowed him to exert as much energy as possible. I enrolled Micah in little league baseball, but the dirt and asthma were not encouragers for Micah to pursue his baseball career further. The dirt caused Micah to have asthma flair ups that become unbearable for him. Since baseball wasn't working, I decided to try soccer. Soccer wasn't a fit either. Regardless of what I enrolled him in, this asthma and allergies were barriers continuously.

I was purely frustrated as a mother. I felt like I've tried everything that I could, too much avail, to give Micah an outlet to exert his energy. He was a child that loved to run, jump, and be as active as possible, but his medical history became his worst enemy.

One morning, as I was driving to work, I accidentally came across a Christian radio show. I was mesmerized by the pastor and his message he was speaking. He stated that God designed us according to His image and uses each of us for His glory. That message made me reflect on the promise that God gave me. *Micah is going to touch millions.* I reflect on that promise this very day, but I knew at that moment it was a sign of something further. As I listened, the pastor continued with his message, I had a gut-wrenching need to visit the church of the pastor that spoke a language that I was familiar with.

You are aware of a past church experience that I have lived through? It was not so pleasant so you could imagine the peace that I had to feel when I was spiritually pulled to visit this church. I made it a point to visit the church the following Sunday. This church was way different from my previous church in Detroit. The moment the kids and I walked through the doors of the church, we were welcomed with opened arms. I was hesitantly waiting to see if the church members would have an issue with the kids – mainly with Micah and Donnie. If you were to tell me to hold my breath, I would have held my breath for a long time. The church members did not see the flaws within the disabilities of the boys. They welcomed my family with open arms.

Micah made friends the very first day we visited the church. He seemed to fit right in with all the other kids. The children's church program was a match for Micah. They kept him active and learning. Micah learned Bible verses and began to find his own spiritual path. He became a praying little something. Micah would never eat without praying. He faithfully prayed every night before going to bed. Even though he was only six years old, Micah truly set the example that we followed in the household; so much so, that we ended each night with a family meeting. Micah loved the Lord at such a young age! He lit up every time we went to church.

One Sunday morning, after church, Micah approached me about a program the church offered. The program was called UPWARD Sports. He and Donnie wanted to sign up for the basketball program. As determined as Micah seemed, I knew Micah knew nothing about basketball let alone knew how to dribble a ball. As a supportive mother, I let them sign up. I was just waiting to see how long it would last. Donnie elected to not continue with the basketball team. The team was beginning to interfere with his martial arts schedule, and he really wanted to stick with his martial arts.

Micah made a choice to keep going with the team. He was a point guard on the team, and it was a sight to see! While everyone else is playing in the game, Micah was on the court doing flips, cartwheels, and spins. Of course, all the other mothers would turn to me, during the games, and ask what was Micah doing? What else could I say? Micah was being Micah.

One day, it was a close game, and it was Micah's turn to enter the game. It was a rule of UPWARD Sports that all players would have a chance to play in every game – regardless of the child's skill level. Micah got in the game, and he did the expected. He turned the ball over. He was not focused as he should have been and everyone was yelling at him. Micah looked so overwhelmed. As each second passed, I became upset. The kid was only seven years old! What were people expecting? I wanted to tell everyone to just calm down and that it will be ok. Micah's teammates took it in stride, and so did the coach. After the game, Micah stated he had fun! His team did end up winning the game.

When I got home that evening, the coach called me to apologize for the behavior of the unruly parents. She also agreed that no child should be yelled at in the manner of what took place, especially at a church function. I agreed. When I spoke with Micah later that day, he stated he did notice the yelling because it was so loud in the gym. Micah was the type of child who could block out noises when he needed to, and he did so during that game. I was just glad that Micah was able to find something that he could stick with.

## Christmas Carols

One day, the kids asked if they could participate in the youth choir at church. They were excited to be a part of the Christmas program. It was also a requirement for all kids to be a part of the youth choir if they wanted to be a part of the Christmas program. I was willing to allow the kids to participate, but I also foresaw the possible challenges. For the kids to be a part of the Christmas program, meant that Micah and Donnie would have to remain focused over long periods of time without me being in their presence. Deep down, I did not want them to sabotage the relationship that we developed with the church. I knew that no matter how much they wanted to do well, their impulsive habits would overcome them. I knew that they had not developed a mechanism in their life yet to better assist them with coping with those urges of impulsivity. I prayed about it and allowed the boys to participate in the Christmas program. When I signed them up, the church informed me that they needed volunteers during the rehearsals. I immediately signed up to volunteer to make sure that I would be available on the sidelines.

During the rehearsals, Micah and Donnie needed minimal correctional prompts. If something came up, I quickly redirect them which limited the necessary interventions. I was so proud of them! Exhibiting restraint and not getting called out due to hyperactive habits was something each of them wanted to do, and they put in the effort to make it work.  Over the years, I worked with Micah ad Donnie to teach them the importance of knowing what possible consequences could be linked to unfavorable behavior.  They both knew that if either one of them acted up, that a consequence would be issued.  The reward this time was for them to be able to sing in the Christmas program.  Both, Micah and Donnie, didn't want to deal with consequences of not being able to sing in the Christmas program.

As the Christmas program approached, the kids wanted to invite their grandmother, aunts, and uncles.  Although neither was a prominent factor in their lives, Donnie and Bessie wanted their mother and father to come to the Christmas program.  The kids and I let the family know that their presence was requested.  I really hoped that they would all show up.  The family dynamic was not so great, even with me living in the same city.  This was a moment for the kids, and I prayed that they were all able to see that.

The kids did great during the Christmas program.  Although their grandmother was the only one to show up, they made the best of the moment, and their hard work paid off.  This was their day!  That was a proud mommy and aunt moment for me.

Later that evening, Micah kept convincing me why I should allow him to become Bill Cosby.  He said he really wanted to be an actor, entertainer, performer, etc.  I promised him I would consider it and let him know.  At that moment, I just really wanted to prepare for the upcoming holidays and spend time with the kids.

As a Christmas Day tradition, the kids and I visited the houses of friends and family or had family and friends come over to our house. On this Christmas Day, the kids opened their gifts that they picked out for themselves. Now you may be wondering why the kids would be opening gifts that they chose for themselves. I can explain. I was never a parent to promote Santa Clause in my household. The kids knew where the gifts really came from – me. When Donnie and Bessie moved in with Micah and me, I began to make it a point to take them shopping individually. It was as if it was our personal one on one time to bond. Raising three kids is a blessing and challenging, altogether, but I also knew the importance of having one on one time with each kid.

The rounds to everyone's houses were full of laughter and fun... Until we made our way to my immediate family's house. My family was talking with the kids and asking them what they received for Christmas. Granted, the kids didn't get much from the family by way of Christmas presents. Donnie told them that he received clothes, a pair of sneakers, and $75 cash. Bessie told them that she received a big doll house, with furniture, and dolls for the doll house. Then it was Micah's turn. He told them that he received a Nintendo DS and two games to go with it. Do you remember when I told you that the kids picked out what they wanted? Well, my family missed that memo. They immediately accused me of showing favoritism towards Micah and not treating Donnie and Bessie fairly. Even if I were to spend the next three hours explaining my case, it would have been useless. I thought this was going to be a day of family and unity. Our family relationship was strained as it is and this was something else that added fuel to the fire.

Again, I was reminded of the lack of support that I didn't have from my family. It truly hurt me to know that the very family that wanted me to take on Donnie and Bessie would accuse me of treating them as if they were children in an orphanage. Oh yeah, my family asked me to take Donnie and Bessie because they knew my character as a mom, a professional, and as a person. If my family really understood the sacrifices that I made personally and professional for Donnie and Bessie maybe they would have other "opinions." I just knew that this was even more of a reason for me to look within my outer circle for the support that I needed as a single mother.

- 42 -

# A Star Is Born!

I found one way to release my frustrations.  Poetry.  I wrote poetry whenever I felt stressed or overwhelmed.  It was as if I had my own personal critique every time I wrote a poem.  Although Micah was seven years old, he was an above average reader.  He would read my poems after I wrote them.  Micah read them no more than three times and would have them memorized.  That wasn't Micah's only amazing ability.  As he recited my poems, he brought them to life.  With every word, Micah knew the motions and facial expressions to suck you in.  It was mesmerizing to watch.   Micah  began  to  perform  for  people  as  a  way  of entertaining them whenever he got bored.  Everywhere we went, people wanted to see him perform a poem.  He would do it at the drop of a hat!

One  day,  I  was  playing  old  school  hip-hop  music  while doing things around the house.  There was a song playing by LL Cool J (Radio), one of my favorite rappers of all time.  After the song was over, to my surprise, Micah knew the chorus and some of the verses.  He started rapping the song around the house as if he had known the song for years.  I knew he wanted to entertain people, but was it really possible for him to have this much talent at such a young age?

I began to think of the promise that God made to me.  *Micah is going to touch millions of people*.  I contacted my sorority sister,

Tasha, and asked if she were aware of any programs in the Milwaukee area that I could have Micah attend to help cultivate his poetry and rapping skills. Tasha immediately proceeded to give me the contact information for Victor Barnett. Victor Barnett is a well-known community activist in the local area. He is the founder of an organization called Running Rebels. Running Rebels is an inner-city program, in Milwaukee, that offers opportunities in a number of areas for youth and young adults. I called Victor and scheduled a meeting with him. I didn't know what to expect, but I knew this would be a step in the right direction to help Micah craft his skills.

I remember the day of the meeting as if it were yesterday. When we arrived, Victor was unavailable at our scheduled appointment time, so we met with one of his representatives until his meeting ended. The representative asked Micah what was it that he did. Micah, a more than confident seven-year-old, held his head high and stated, "I am a poet and a rapper!" Micah then asked the representative if he wanted to see him perform. The rep nodded with approval and Micah proceeded to step into his element.

> *People everywhere check out my story, about how I proclaimed all of my glory. I was riding my bike down the street one day when something just totally took my breath away. Well, I turned around and paused for a second, when all of a sudden, something dropped from*

*heaven. I didn't know what to do, it was a terrible fright,*
*I turned back around, and I saw a Mic!  A Mic for me,*
*who Micah B.  Man, I was so happy, I did not know what*
*to do, it just appeared like somebody knew.  I picked up*
*the Mic, and I said a few words, I was the best that the*
*people had heard!*

Everyone in the office gathered around and started to clap for Micah.  Some said, in shock, "Lil' Dude is really good!"  Micah had no fear.  He then asked if they wanted to hear him recite poetry. They all nodded yes, in unison, and Micah proceeded to recite his poem.

*Dad,*
*I'm writing you this letter, and I really wonder,*
*Does it truly matter?*
*Is it something I have done?*
*Was it my mom?*
*Or did you just choose not to love me?*
*Dads are supposed to love their children*
*Just like moms*
*God gave you a chance to blossom*
*But you chose not to trust Him*
*You can have all the wealth in the world*
*But without a family*
*It means nothing*
*That's why*

*I forgive you, Dad*

*For what you have done*

*The pain you have caused*

*The years you have missed*

*The many times I wished*

*That I had a dad*

*The moments I felt sad…*

Again, everyone started clapping and telling Micah how good he was. At that point, Victor Barnett entered the room and introduced himself to Micah. Micah exchanged the introduction. Victor asked his representative what he thought of Micah. The young man looked at Victor and exclaimed, "He is great!"

Victor gave Micah and me a tour of the facility. Throughout the tour, Micah was smiles from ear to ear. He was also running all over the place, touching everything in sight. Victor did not seem to mind. He allowed Micah to be a kid. Victor welcomed Micah with open arms.

Micah's countenance changed when Victor took us up some stairs that led to a recording studio. Micah's eyes lit up. This was the first time I had ever seen Micah give total attention to ANYONE! Victor was explaining all the equipment to Micah. Micah just sat there, and he listened. Micah did not interrupt Victor. He did ask questions at the end of the tour. Micah really wanted to go into the booth to record, but Victor told him he would get his chance in the future.

Micah wasn't the only one that was sold after the tour. I was amazed that Micah was now being offered the opportunity to really live out his dreams. I could only thank God for leading me to make the call to Tasha. Victor totally had my buy-in on how awesome the Running Rebels would be – not just for Micah, but also for Donnie and Bessie. The Running Rebels offered programs that addressed all of the kids' interest. I needed all the resources that were available for them since they were getting older.

# Is This the Remedy?

Micah was serious about his craft, and he wanted to make sure that he was able to become better as an entertainer. He started performing at open mics throughout the Milwaukee area at that age of seven years old. He was making a name for himself as a poet and rapper. Micah was winning so many contests, in his age group, that I had to stop him from competing and only appear as a guest performer. By the age of eight, Micah was performing in venues with some of Milwaukee's well-known poets: Dasha Kelly, Dan Vaughn, Kwabena Nixon, just to name a few.

Micah was attending a Christian Academy at this point in his life. His school had a forensic debate team, and he was intrigued with what they did. When it was time for enrollment, Micah auditioned for his grade category, and he made the team! Micah became so good that he qualified for the state competition, during his first year on the team. For his state performance, Micah chose to perform *The Boy Who Cried Wolf*, by Randy Johnson. I think I was nervous for Micah and me both. As in any state competition, the children were separated by their grade and performed according to the last name. Micah was fourth in line to compete. They allowed the parents to remain in the rooms for the competition, so it was great to see everyone's facial expression as Micah performed. The first three students performed and the judges completed their scorecards. Now it was Micah's turn to perform. Micah stood up confidently and walked to the front of the room. He introduced himself and the title of his performance piece. I watched Micah in awe. He was in a league of his own. After Micah had finished his piece, the judges asked for a recess so they could leave the room and have a private discussion. At that moment, I thought to myself that Micah probably should not have been in that competition because he was way too advanced for the group that he competed against. The judges re-entered the room and proceeded with the competition. Ultimately, Micah received the highest score and honors for his grade level.

Although I had Micah involved in church and poetry, on a regular basis, his behavior continued to be a concern for his teachers. He was taking medication, and I had him participating in activities of his choice, but the focus during the school day was minimal. Micah really liked his teachers. I remember meeting with his principal and teacher about setting up a token reward system for Micah at school. I knew Micah responded well to immediate tangibles. That was why he did so well in the recording studio and at church. He saw the church and the studio as two places that he didn't want to miss out on. I never punished Micah and not allow him to go to church. It was the extra, fun church activities that Micah didn't want to miss out on. I needed to find a way for Micah to feel the same way about school. The

Principal's plan included Micah having the opportunity to have lunch with his teacher when earned enough award tokens to do so. We purposefully explain the system for Micah, and he was onboard with the plan.

The plan was successful! After the implementation of the reward system, the previous communication patterns from Micah's teachers changed. Thankfully, Micah's school was very patient when it came to Micah's hyperactive habits. After much improvement at school, Micah approached me after school, one day, asked if he could join the wrestling team. Talk about a kid that had confidence. I shouldn't have been surprised by this time. Micah was confident in his ability to do anything, despite his small stature. I also shouldn't have been surprised, only because I encouraged Micah to have faith in God and to believe in himself. I agreed to let Micah try out and guess what?? He made the team! Call it favor or good luck, but Micah was never turned away from anything that he tried out for.

His first wrestling meet was so interesting. I didn't know much about wrestling, but I quickly learned that it was a serious contact sport. It was also a sport that required a lot of discipline. The boys had to start and stop at the commands of the referees. I wondered if this was something that Micah was ready for. Micah participated in his first match. He wrestled against boys his size and weight - regardless of their age or grade. Micah's coach told me that he did good for his first wrestling meet, but I really did not understand much about wrestling or the scoring process. I supported Micah regardless of my lack of knowledge for this new venture. I just wanted Micah to be happy.

At home, I implemented a structured environment for Micah, but it still exposed some challenges. My health issues were still on an unpredictable seesaw. Micah's energy was more present than my own. Talk about an interesting combination between a mother and son.

There was a YMCA a few miles from our house. I decided to enroll the kids in all programs that were available to them. They really wanted to take swimming lessons, so I added that to their list of activities. I felt it was important for each of them to learn to swim, especially because of Micah and Donnie's hyperactivity. Additionally, swimming was a great form of exercise. This YMCA had a humongous slide, which the boys enjoyed. I would watch them from the glass window outside the pool on the slide, and there they were smiling, laughing, and having a ball!

As a parent, I had ammunition and motivation to get Micah to make an extra effort in limiting his hyperactive outbursts. There was so much for him to look forward to with all of the activities that he was tied to. Each activity was some type of reward for Micah. He had choices in what he wanted to do.

It got to a point where Micah was overly busy with activities, and he was also getting paid to perform. As a mother, I felt that there was a solid structure in place that allowed Micah to see that tangible rewards should be more than a motivation. All of what he was involved in were activities that helped Micah become the person that he was destined to be. Yes, some of the activities were in place to help manage with his hyperactive habits, but even those activities were a true benefit to Micah.

Micah started to set goals to record a CD. He and I both knew that recording a CD wouldn't happen overnight, but to Micah, it was another reward to work towards. He was so excited about the thoughts of recording a CD that he opened up a bank account with the money that he started to earn. I didn't have a full plan on behalf of Micah's CD, but I knew that I needed to continuously show him support and walk the path with him.

# REFLECTION MOMENTS

1. What do you love most about being a mother?

_____

_____

_____

_____

_____

_____

2. Name one trait that your child possesses and can
   be considered as a negative trait by society.

_____

_____

_____

_____

_____

_____

3. Identify a strength that you admire most about your child.

_____

_____

_____

_____

4. How many programs can you identify for your child that he/she can benefit from?

_____

_____

_____

_____

5. How often do you find yourself communicating with your child's teacher(s)? For what reasons?

_____

_____

_____

# NOTES

## Overnight Success

Do you believe that there are no coincidences in life? I do. I am also a firm believer that certain "doors" open at the right time in life as well. It was not a coincidence that I called a friend who recommended that I reach out to Victor. Since meeting Victor, our lives changed. By the time Micah was nearing the end of the third grade, he was more than well-known throughout the Milwaukee area by his moniker, Lil' Dude. He was semi-famous. Micah made a name for himself as a performer. It was as if everyone knew who Micah was.

Victor paired Micah with a mentor, by the name of Ward. Ward worked diligently with Micah to get him prepared to record his first song. Who would've thought that at the age of eight, my son would be in a recording studio to record his first song! Ward was not only involved in Micah's life, but he was also interested in his well-being. One day, while in the studio, Ward sat Micah down and had a heart to heart conversation. Ward told Micah to always be good at what he does. Because Micah was so young, people always thought he was "cute." Ward explained to Micah that as he got older, people would expect for him to be a good performer – not a cute performer. From that day forward, Micah's outlook on his future changed. He knew, furthermore, what he wanted to do in life and that was to be the best performer he could be. Micah rehearsed and practiced every possible moment.

Ward wasn't soft with Micah. He expected the best. It seemed the harder Ward was with Micah, the better Micah did. Micah didn't back down nor did he whine about how much work was being required of him.

After long days of rehearsing, the big day finally arrived. Micah was excited, and so were the team that helped him at the studio. When I arrived at the studio, everyone was excited. They immediately sat me down and had me listen to Micah's first recording. I listened to Micah's first recording intently. Although he had a tiny voice, his words were mind blowing! I was so proud of this kid. Micah was living out his dreams at such a young age. I had to step back and reflect on where he came from. A kid that wasn't expected to live was now living and speaking life into a microphone. Once his song was done blasting in the speakers, Micah leaned over and asked, "Mommy, do you like my song?" I couldn't answer right away because I was speechless. Micah knew my answer by the big smile that I had on my face.

For the remainder of the school year, Micah performed his recorded song at various schools, youth facilities, parks, festivals, and other special events. Micah was motivated by the way other kids looked up to him. His teachers also had a different point of view of him too. Micah was no longer seen as the "bad" student always getting into trouble. After recording his song, his grades started to improve too. Micah was improving academically, but his behavioral habits and outbursts continued to occur. His asthma also continued to limit his ability to fulfill some of his performance engagements and commitments, but everyone seemed to understand.

Although Micah was becoming famous in his own right, he never let success get in the way of him wanting to be a little boy. In October of that year, Micah turned nine years old. He said he wanted to have an all-boys birthday party. He said he also wanted a magician. At first, I thought what harm can a magician and a few little boys do. Micah had other plans. He took it upon himself to invite thirty boys to his party. And guess what? All of their parents confirmed for them to attend. Did you hear what I said? Thirty boys confirmed for a birthday party! What in the world was I going to do for thirty boys at a birthday party that was to take place at my house? I needed reinforcements, and I needed them fast. I leaned on the help of friends to host the party. We cleared out all of the living furniture and made other arrangements to accommodate the boys. Imagine a room full of nine-year-old boys, in one place, with a magician. Micah told me this was his best birthday ever! The magician was so engulfed in his performance that he ended up giving me two hours for the price of one hour. After the magic show, the boys sang happy birthday to Micah and ate food. Boy, did they eat! They ate hot dogs, French fries, ice cream, and cake. The food was Micah's favorite food at the time.

Opportunities for Micah kept rolling in. The United States Department of Justice hosted a competition and Micah decided to enter the contest. At that point, Micah still wasn't writing his own songs as of yet. Victor was able to enlist a group of teenagers, who participated in the Running Rebels music program, to help Micah write a song. The two teenagers went by the monikers of Young Oki and Yung Legend. They worked with Micah, who was going by the moniker of Lil' Dude at the time. When it was time to record the song, Micah went to the studio and recorded the song in one take. Who records a song, at his age?! Micah was determined to give it his all, and he did. The song was an energetic song that best suited Micah's personality and rapping style. The song was entered into the competition, and Micah ended up winning! Everyone at Running Rebels was happy for Micah. I was more than happy for Micah. He was going after his dreams with all of his heart.

One of the prizes, for the competition, was the chance to go to a professional recording studio to record a song. Micah received a limousine ride to the studio, and it was recorded. After he professionally recorded the song, it was featured on the radio, television, and public transportation. Micah was also interviewed at a local hip hop radio station where his song was played. I felt like Micah was well on his way, even though he was only nine years old.

During the summer, Micah honed his rapping skills. He was acting in small plays, was signed to a local talent agency, performed throughout the city, and prepared to record his first full album. Micah even performed at his uncle Drel's wedding in Dallas, Texas. To improve his writing skills, Micah starting writing songs with his cousin, Derrick. To ensure that he was still living a "normal life," I enrolled Micah at a well-known basketball camp at Marquette University where he was able to meet and hang out with Dwayne Wade. Also, when basketball camp ended, he attended a day camp at the YMCA. Micah's behaviors remained sporadic, at best, but I knew he was making the necessary behavioral efforts as much as he could. As a rising fourth grader, this was enough to keep him occupied and busy.

## <u>What is Wrong with This Picture?</u>

At the start of the school year, I Micah transferred to a local well-known charter school in Milwaukee.  At this point, critical changes in his behavior took a turn for the worst.  He began fighting with peers which, was never an issue in the past.  He wasn't completing any school work.  Micah was just always playing with his peers and making paper airplanes.  I immediately scheduled a conference with his teacher to discuss what could cause this type of change in his behavior.  I spoke with Micah too, but he shrugged his shoulders - not giving a reason.  As a parent, I was more than dumbfounded and wanted answers immediately. I knew that a change in his environment could be a contributing factor, but he had experienced change before and nothing this drastic had occurred in such a short period of time.

I visited his class and observed the classroom for more than one reason.  I needed to see the environment from Micah's point of view.   I also needed to address my observations, from a parent's standpoint, with Micah's teacher.  My observation time was startling – to say the least.  The teacher had the classroom arranged in a way where all the boys sat in the back of the classroom near the door, while the girls sat in the front of the classroom.  It was not conducive for Micah because I have always requested to have him sit in the front due to his ADHD diagnosis. If Micah was distracted, I wondered what the other students were going through. Micah was the type of kid that got distracted easily. It did not take much effort on anyone's part to distract him from the obvious. Micah's impulsive behaviors were happening on a daily basis, and unless something changed, his behaviors would probably not change much. Please understand, I was never one to make excuses for Micah, but I also had to advocate on his behalf when things were obviously setting Micah up to fail. No slight to his teacher. She may have just stuck with something that worked for her and her classes, over the years, but this was Micah that we were dealing with. I knew my child would not excel in the current class environment that was in place.

Although I knew that things weren't "right" at school, Micah did receive consequences for his inexcusable behaviors at school. He needed to understand that he still has control over his behavior. The punishment did not resolve behavior issues, although I know he was trying. The ongoing discipline related to his behaviors at school was compromising the healthy relationship that existed between Micah and me as mother and son. I felt helpless. No matter what I did, it felt as if no one wanted to listen. The teachers felt they knew more than I. They stuck with the notion that Micah knew "how to act right." One teacher had the audacity to tell me that Micah sought special attention because he was on TV and was well known. I was more than taken aback. It was more than evident that the teachers did not understand his disability. But was it truly my responsibility to teach them?

I found myself going to his school almost on a daily basis. The teachers at Micah's school all said in one accord that Micah was so polite, but he does not listen to anyone. What sense did that make? Keep in mind, Micah really wanted to do his best in school, but he was so easily distracted. No one could truly understand how a child, who had accomplished so much at such an early age, not have the attention span to focus in the classroom. I needed empathy from them. I needed them to walk in Micah's shoes and understand why he acted out.

I advocated, endlessly, for Micah to be able to sit in front of the class. Eventually, the teacher arranged the classroom so Micah could sit in the front of the class. Micah's disruptive behavior and impulsivity began to decrease drastically. In all honesty, all I asked of the school was to use a person-centered approach in supporting Micah in the class. He was a student who was motivated to learn, and he loved school, but all everyone could see was a child who did not think he had to listen. That was an incorrect assessment of my son. I had to make them see who my son was through my eyes and through his disabilities. In the end, I was successful in advocating for his accommodations and his grades improved along with his behaviors.

# The Album

As I guided Micah back on track, we began to search for producers for his first album. As an agreement, Micah work on recording his first album once his behavior became up to par. Not only at school, but also at home. Can I tell you this? I knew nothing about putting together an album. Micah wanted to call the album *Like Me*. That's all that I knew was for sure. I didn't know what to look for in a producer. I didn't know how to get CDs reproduced. I knew nothing. I leaned on Victor and Ward for guidance to help Micah achieve this next milestone. I recruited Derrick, along with Micah's teenage writing mentors, to be the official writers for the project. A local Milwaukee producer, Shady Dude, was chosen to produce the album. It took Micah eight months to complete the album - from beginning to end. His excitement, while working on the project was priceless! He was even more excited to work towards something that his mentors had already accomplished. Astonishingly, I didn't fully fund this project. Micah insisted on helping to finance the project with his earnings from his gigs.

Micah completed his album in July 2005. To launch his album, Micah partnered with the Milwaukee Summer of Peace initiative another mentor, Viva Fidel. He participated in press conferences and live interviews to spread help promote the overall mission of the initiative. Micah also met with the local representatives and media. Most of all, he was able to do what he loved best – entertain. Micah performed in front of thousands of people. The Summer of Peace was the perfect partnership for Micah. Their message lined up with the message that Micah promoted in his music.

At the time Micah's album dropped, Milwaukee was known as and still is a high crime city. Micah delivered a message of love and fun. He wanted people to get along. He also wanted the violence in the city to stop. I remember Micah telling me one day, that he was tired of all the killings! That became Micah's message. After the release of his album, local radio stations throughout Milwaukee interviewed Micah. His momentum was high, and everyone was getting a piece of Lil' Dude mania. He was selling t-shirts, hats, posters, and albums.

As Micah's mother, it was important to let him know that I was proud of him and that I supported him every step of the way. Micah received continuous encouragement from me. I wanted him to know that he could always trust me regardless of any situation.

At the age of nine, Micah felt that he was a big boy and I wanted to allow him more freedom, but under the right circumstances. Micah was still dealing with severe asthmatic symptoms, impulsivity, and hyperactivity, so it was critical that I put him in situations to be successful. I knew that I wanted to build his self-esteem. I wanted Micah always to feel good about who he was regardless of how he entered the world or his disabilities.

# REFLECTION MOMENTS

1. In what areas do you advocate for your child?

_____

_____

_____

_____

2. How do you advocate for your child?

_____

_____

_____

_____

3. Explain a moment where your child went above and beyond, which ultimately surprised you.

_____

_____

_____

_____

**4. What is one "flaw" that people point out continuously about your child?**

_____

_____

_____

_____

_____

**5. Does your child's school provide student-centered support?**

_____

_____

_____

_____

_____

# NOTES

# NEW BEGINNINGS

## Bitter Sweet

As things progressed, I knew that change was near. I just didn't know what the change was until it was put on my heart to leave Milwaukee. I didn't hesitate with making this move a reality, because of many factors. My family dynamic didn't change from the day that I moved back to Milwaukee. Most family members felt that I was spending way too much time grooming Micah for success and not paying "attention" to Donnie and Bessie. Keep in mind, Donnie and Bessie were still living with me. Between the three children, I always made it a point to treat them as individuals. Donnie was not interested in the things that Micah was interested in. Donnie was involved with the Sigma Beta Club and learning to DJ at the Running Rebels. Bessie just wanted to be a "typical" girl. She spent most of her time with my mother, her paternal grandmother. She was also involved with extra curriculum activities at her school. They were all doing what they loved. I never chose to force a particular lifestyle on either one of them. I never made it a point to disregard Donnie and Bessie just because Micah was accomplishing things in life. I did everything that I set my heart to do for each one of them.

Another reason why I didn't hesitate to make a move was the crime rate that was increasingly becoming disturbing. Every time I turned around, it seemed like someone was either getting murdered or going to jail for committing a crime. It was an environment that I didn't want the kids to grow up in. I knew that I could only shield them but from so much. If I had anything to do with it, I would always give them the best environment the best way that I could.

Once I knew the decision was final to move, I sat all three kids down and told them what the decision was. Micah was excited about a new change. Donnie and Bessie, on the other hand, wanted to stay. They wanted to be around family, even though relationships were rocky. They were especially rocky with their own birth parents, but for whatever reason, they wanted to stay. It hurt my heart to know that they wanted to stay and not leave. I took into consideration their age and ultimately honored their request. I knew in my heart that I would eventually regret my decision, but I wanted to hope for the best. My mother offered to care for Donnie and Bessie. Although I was still their legal guardian, I made the decision for them to reside my mother and prepared to still provide for them while living in another state.

There was a lot to prepare for with this move. Where would we live? Where would Micah go to school? Would Micah continue to grow in the entertainment industry? All of these questions became my thought process as I prepared for a move. I knew we were moving to Atlanta, Georgia, but I knew a plan needed to be put into place.

Before coming to Atlanta, I reached out to a well-known talent agent, Joy Pervis. I did not know the first thing about getting him into acting or modeling, other than my brief experience in Milwaukee. I telephoned Mrs. Pervis on many occasions and left messages. I sent her videos of Micah. I sent articles. I sent everything that I felt would help paint the picture of Micah being an entertainer. Please understand, Mrs. Pervis has worked with some phenomenal child actresses and actors. Micah was a nobody in the context of the entertainment world. As the calls and messages became unanswered, I still didn't' give up. I chose to persist because I knew this was something that Micah wanted to do. He wanted to be an entertainer, and I was his only advocate to help make it happen. Some felt that Micah becoming famous would be impossible, but to me it was possible! One day, I called Joy Pervis, and she answered the phone. I was shocked. I was not expecting her to answer the phone. I was expecting to leave the rehearsed voicemail that I have left many times before. I introduced myself and then explained why I was calling. At first, Mrs. Pervis did not have any clue of who I was. Nor was she able to confirm if she received the items that I previously sent her. That didn't stop me. I just kept talking. The more I spoke to her the more she became engaged. She finally asked if Micah was that "little rapper." Finally! I knew I had her. Micah did make an impression. I tried to hide my excitement as I did confirm that Micah was the "little rapper." She wanted to know when we were getting to Atlanta and I told her sometime within the next couple of months. Mrs. Pervis said that once we get settled in Atlanta, she would make it a point to meet with us.

I was hoping that the transition from leaving Milwaukee would go as smooth as possible. I sold my house not knowing where we would live. I just knew that we were leaving. I wanted to "travel" lightly so I sold what I could from the house and left the rest, hoping that my family members would do right as they promised. I left my car with my mother so she can have transportation while caring for Donnie and Bessie. In me doing so, I was without a car, so I had to rent a car when we first moved to Atlanta. We were moving to an unfamiliar city where I only knew three people that were not family members. When we arrived in Atlanta, I made the decision to stay at an Extended Stay America Hotel for a while. A lot was happening all at once, and I needed to make decisions that were "simple."

Although Micah and I left Milwaukee, family issues still followed. Before leaving, I made sure Donnie and Bessie was registered for school and had the clothes and resources they needed. I also made arrangements to send money to my mother on a regular schedule. Little did I know, that as I was making plans to move, a family member reported me to the child welfare agency. The same agency in which I was employed before me leaving the state. The accusation was that I abandoned Donnie and Bessie to move to another city in favor of Micah. You could only imagine how devastated I was. While also dealing with this,

I also had to deal with things going array with the belongings that I left in Milwaukee. I would have never imagined that I would have to deal with deceit from those that were "closest" to me. I was investigated, as a guardian, even while recently moving to Atlanta. At some point during the investigation, the case worker put two and two together. It came to light all that I have done for Donnie and Bessie, even before moving to Atlanta. The case worker apologized for the trouble that I had to go through because of what took place. She commended me for still taking care of two children that had living parents, even while living in another state.

I went through a time of being depressed after the family chaos. I replayed everything that I did for Donnie and Bessie in my mind. I was searching for the areas of where I may have missed it, while they were in my care. Was I always perfect? No! But I can definitely say that I sacrificed for Donnie and Bessie no different than I sacrificed for Micah. I treated them all the same. I was never dependent on government assistance and never received one cent in child support from either parent. All of their needs were met. They had the best of everything. I encouraged them to excel and live life for their dreams and for themselves. I ultimately had to realize that this was a situation that I couldn't control. I couldn't control the actions of others that had hang-ups with me – for whatever reason. Or with Micah for that matter. Micah and I were living in a new city, and I had to make the best of it for Micah. I loved my niece and nephew like they were my children. I knew that I could not make them move to Atlanta and have them resent me for it. It was a truly difficult decision, but I felt I needed to leave the city to grow personally and professionally. Milwaukee wouldn't have only stunted the children's growth, but it was stunting my growth. I made the decision that I thought was best for us all, but I still regretted the decision that I made by allowing Donnie and Bessie to stay with my mother.

# In Search of New Beginnings

I registered Micah in DeKalb County Path Academy, which was a DeKalb County Public Charter School near Oglethorpe University. He was in the fifth grade and attending a year-round middle school. I really had to be mindful that this was a huge transition for Micah. Yes, he was excited about the change, but I knew that change sometimes triggered certain behaviors. When we left Milwaukee, Micah was leaving a place where people knew him. Not for his disabilities, but for his talents. Now that we moved to Atlanta, Micah literally had to start over to build a name for himself in the entertainment industry.

The moment we arrived in Atlanta, I went to the library to use the internet. I needed to find out everything that I could about the city of Atlanta. I made a note of every open mic that Micah could attend, and we started to attend them. There were some limitations, given Micah's age. He was only nine years old and was allowed at certain events. We quickly found out that Atlanta was much different from Milwaukee. Eventually, we found our niche! Once Micah was able to perform on a regular basis in Atlanta, people began changing their mindset and saw what Micah had to offer as an entertainer. By the age of ten, he was performing throughout Atlanta at various open mics, festivals, and elementary schools. We utilized the barber shops and malls, as venues, to pass out business cards and CDs. We also used Myspace and Craigslist to market Micah as an entertainer.

When we finally got settled, I scheduled a meeting with Joy Pervis. Micah did a short read for her. Before I knew it, we were signing a contract with Joy Pervis! Micah started with small print modeling gigs and voice over jobs, but the fact was he was working! It didn't matter how big or small the job was to Micah. What mattered most was that he was doing what he loved. There were times that Micah was not chosen for certain jobs or roles. I used those moments to boost his morale the best way possible. I would usually tell him that they were looking for a Mercedes and he was a BMW. He would smile in agreement, knowing that he would have a shot at more opportunities. Micah was a child that had thick skin, and I was more than thankful for that.

## Different Environment Same Behavior

At school, Micah was doing great academically, but he always seemed to attract the wrong kind of crowd. The crowds that he got tangled up with always seemed to play during class and not stay focused. Of course, I was at the school meeting with teachers to discuss his challenges on a regular basis.

Because Micah was getting older, I had to take into consideration the changes that he may be dealing with medically. I found him a pediatrician who was marvelous. He tried different medications for Micah until we found the right dosage to assist with his ADHD diagnosis. What I found interesting was that he was prescribed Singulair for his asthma, since Claritin was deemed as an over the counter medication and the insurance would not cover it. Boy, was there a rude awakening when Micah started to take his new medicine! Once he started the Singulair, his hyperactive habits increased! I did not want to increase his dosage of Concerta, which was prescribed for ADHD. I needed answers, and I continued to seek them out. After speaking with his doctor and researching his medication, I discovered a side effect of Singulair was increased hyperactivity. I wish I knew that before agreeing to put him on Singulair, but it was a lesson learned. Therefore, I managed his medication and purchased Claritin and kept it on hand when needed. Micah's nebulizer medicine had a similar side effect, but I knew that was an as needed prescription. I was put in a dilemma because I wanted to do what was best for my son, but at what cost?

Now that it was only Micah, I could pour all my energy into ensuring he could reach his dream. I had to sacrifice for the sake of his future. Micah was my child, and he was my responsibility. We kept up a regular schedule of attending networking events, going to concerts, meeting celebrities, and performing all over Atlanta. Every time an opportunity presented itself, we made the best of it. Micah was on cloud nine, and most that interacted with him were unaware of his disabilities. They just saw Micah for who he was and not his disabilities. Micah made friends everywhere he went.

By the time Micah was in the sixth grade, I had found myself disciplining Micah much more than I ever had to do so in the past. He was developing his independence. He also had his peer group who was extremely influential. I understood that, as a social worker, but I wanted him to experience the good with the bad. Just not at the cost of his education. I knew Micah had disabilities, and I knew that he needed the proper tools to be successful such as medication management, structure, and discipline. As a parent, my rules were strict and I made sure structure was implemented on a daily basis. I knew he needed those things in place, continuously, if I expected him to succeed. Micah received consequences, physical discipline, and participated in community service. Many times, the physical discipline did not change his behaviors. Therefore, it became obsolete for the most part.

When I was a child, I was in a special education resource room due to my behavior and reading level. I received physical punished at home and school due to those reasons. I needed to try harder and listen to the teacher. I felt I was trying and I did my best to listen. Eventually, the school conducted a vision screening and realized that I could not see well. Now, thirty plus years later and I still wear glasses. The tool I needed was glasses. I could not see the chalkboard from my seat without glasses. I did not want to look *dumb* in front of my peers, so I acted out. I could not see the words in the book, so it limited my ability to read. When I watched TV, at home, I stood or sat directly in front of it because I could not see from far back. Imagine if I went to school my entire life without the proper tools so I could have been successful. My tool was a simple pair of eyeglasses. Sometimes, as parents, we need to provide our children with the tools they need to be successful in life regardless of what the world thinks or believes. We are experts when it comes to our child. When it came to Micah, I knew that some tools worked with some things, but I may have had to try new things in other situations.

## Make the Changes That Make Sense

It became clear that some things needed to change with Micah's schedule. Between him being at the studio, acting and performing, going to a brick and mortar school just wasn't working. I needed an option that would give Micah the opportunity to complete his school work while pursuing his dreams. I decided to homeschool Micah as he transitioned into the seventh grade. Initially, he was excited. Micah's thinking was that he would be able to sleep and watch TV whenever he wanted to. He was in for a rude awakening because of my expectations, regarding his education, were way much higher than attending a brick and mortar school.

Even while being homeschooled, we still made time for things outside of his entertainment career. Micah was enrolled in acting class, and he went to weekly swimming classes. We took weekly field trips, and I required him to attend a weekly fitness boot camp. Micah even had to conduct research at the library one hour a day. Once he completed his education and personal growth obligations, he was then allowed to do things that he considered to be fun and leisure. Micah also participated in UPWARD Sports at a local church. There was no doubt that he had a daily structure in his life. There were not many opportunities for him to get into trouble. I knew that it was important for him to have a peer group and that is why he participated in so many activities.

As parents, we must realize when a change needs to be made in the lives of our children. We may end up questioning ourselves. Are we making the right decisions? Will things become worse with the change? There are many questions that we may ask ourselves, but we ultimately have to make the changes that make sense. Some people may question you as you make certain decisions. They can make you even feel inadequate. At the end of the day, you have to make the changes that you know will be beneficial in the long run. If anyone disagrees with your decisions, take it with a grain of salt and remain confident that you know your children and what is needed for their success.

## Mentors in Abundance

As Micah continued to participate in events throughout Atlanta, we started connecting with positive male role models who took an interest in Micah, as a person. One of the first people we encountered was Rodney L. Rodney owned a business, and we utilized his services for CD duplication. Before we knew it, we formed a lasting friendship. Rodney and Micah also bonded through a mentoring relationship. Rodney gave us the ins and outs of the music business in Atlanta. He also gave us the much-needed knowledge to expand Micah's career. I was more than grateful for our relationship with Rodney.

One night, Micah was performing at an open mic in the Auburn Avenue area at a local coffee shop. After Micah's performance, another poet approached me asking if I knew Christopher "Cocktails." He stated if I did not know him, I needed to make it a point to know him. I made it a point to research Christopher "Cocktails." I found out what events he was hosting and attending. I made it a point to attend the events that Micah was allowed to attend. I eventually found the right opportunity to make a connection with him. Once Micah and him met each other, they hit it off right then and there. It was a magical connection. Christopher remains a permanent staple in Micah's life and a much-needed mentor.

It seemed as if everyone that I encountered secretly knew that Micah needed all of the mentors that he could have. Another mentor that came highly recommended was a poet named Abyss. The first-time Micah heard Abyss perform poetry, was the day Micah fell in love with poetry. Micah was exposed to poetry before, but this time it was different. After the event, Micah talked about how he thought Abyss was the greatest poet he ever heard. That's all he talked about during the ride home. I knew I had to include Abyss in Micah's life based on Micah's enthusiasm. Micah needed an Abyss in his life. Micah and Abyss immediately connected and he's been a surrogate uncle to Micah ever since.

The list could go on regarding the mentors that were and still are a part of Micah's life. To date, Micah accumulated close to forty mentors in Atlanta alone. Each one of them played a significant role in his life during some of Micah's most difficult and rewarding times. Whether it was music, acting, leadership, male bonding, opportunities, learning to drive, or just relief for me – they were there. There were plenty of people that showed an "interest" in Micah, but I knew which ones truly had the heart for Micah. Did I encounter people that had certain motives? Yes, but as a parent, I was still in control of who played a part in Micah's life. I knew that everyone wouldn't be a great "fit" for Micah and I was ok with that. I don't regret the decisions that were made in the long run.

## Everyone Has a Hero

I first thought moving to Atlanta would create a setback for Micah, but that was not the case. Once the opportunities started flowing, it seemed as if they wouldn't stop. Micah had a publicist when he was only eleven! He performed with Arrested Development at Milwaukee's Summerfest, and he met his hero, KRS-One, a legendary rap artist. His publicist at the time, Tambria Peeples, was in New York for VH1 Hip Hop Honors where she told KRS-One about one of his biggest fans - Micah. KRS-One was probably thinking to himself what business does an eleven-year-old have knowing anything about him. When Micah was about eight years old, I took him to African World Festival. KRS-One was a headliner act for the event. Micah was amazed at his lyrical talent and gravitated towards KRS-One's impact within the history of Hip-Hop. After seeing KRS-One perform at the festival, Micah saw him on TV. That's all Micah could talk about at that time – how great of an artist KRS-One was. Micah had other favorite artists, but at that time KRS-One was his most favorite.

Once KRS-One heard about Micah, he wanted to meet him. Tambria called me, one Sunday afternoon, to inform me that KRS-One was in Atlanta and he wanted to meet Micah. We wanted this meet-up with KRS-One to be a surprise for Micah.

We planned to take Micah to meet KRS-One during the taping of a music video. Upon arrival, Micah walks into the room, and there sits KRS-One. Micah became silent, and tears began to flow down his face. As a mother, all I could do was smile. KRS-One will always have my respect! He made a lasting impression on my child at such a young age. When Micah thought that was it, Rick Ross the rapper walked into the room and greeted Micah with open arms.

Micah met his hero the moment he met KRS-One. Micah was never star struck, growing up as a child. Before meeting KRS-One, he met a lot of other celebrities. Those celebrities just didn't have an impact on Micah the way KRS-One did. KRS-One ultimately invited Micah to participate in the *Stop the Violence* Campaign. KRS-One also linked Micah up with other hip-hop artists - asking for nothing in return. The love KRS-One showed my son left me speechless. Micah's life revolved around hip-hop. He just didn't love hip-hop. Micah was and still is a representation of hip-hop.

## Priceless Opportunities and More Changes

Micah CD was doing well in sales, but he was getting older. I talked to local disc jockeys (DJs), and they recommended that Micah do a mixtape since that was the trend amongst other hip-hop artists. At the time, not many artists Micah's age had a mixtape. Again, I was advised of something that was foreign to me. I've listened to plenty of mixtapes, but I was never in the position to have to produce one. I took to Craigslist and Myspace so we could produce a mixtape. I found a local producer, Gamble, on Craigslist and a local up and coming DJ, DJ Kutt Throat, on Myspace. The rest was history. While producing the mixtape, I set up interviews with local radio stations to promote the project. Eventually, Micah hosted his own radio show! The show was called *Just Kidding Radio,* and it broadcasted on the local am airwaves on Saturday mornings in Atlanta.

During this time, Micah was producing a mixtape, hosting his radio show and still playing with his UPWARD basketball team. You would think that things would've slowed down, but that was an understatement. Micah auditioned to open up for John Legend and Pattie Labelle, and guess what? He was selected to open up at Phillips Arena with some of Atlanta's local youth artists. If you think that would be enough, it wasn't. Micah auditioned for a nationally known TV network, BET. At the time, BET was producing an original sitcom television show called

Somebodies. Micah auditioned to open up for the major artists and BET around the same timeframe. He was selected for both!

Micah was originally supposed to be on set for the TV show, Somebodies, for one day. Before I knew it, Micah had a reoccurring role on the TV show. Throughout the TV experience, Micah stayed true to Micah. He was being himself. He was fearless. Everyone loved Micah and the energy he brought to the table.

Micah was a pre-teen beating the odds of survival. He seemed unstoppable and looked as though he was ready to conquer the world. Micah was touring the Southeast region by way of the *Sounds of Knowledge Tour*. Still performing throughout the Atlanta region, Micah acquired his own band, the Branches, making him even more attractive. He hosted family events, participated in community events and promoted his mixtape. At the age of twelve, Micah was doing a lot.

Even with all the success that Micah was experiencing, Micah approached me, one day, asking if he can join a home schooling group that will allow him to interact with other students. The solution was easy since I knew of a homeschooling group that his band members attended. At first, Micah seemed to like it, but Micah began having issues with focusing and remaining on task. He was around his friends all day and after school. It made it difficult for him to focus when it was required for him to do so. I still had to keep in mind that Micah was immature for his age. At times, his peers would be "mature," Micah was one to joke around and get into trouble.

This was truly a time that I needed to lean on Micah's mentors. Abyss did an excellent job in getting him to re-focus his attention on what it needed to be. In looking back on things, I sometimes wondered if Micah wanted to continue pursuing his entertainment goals given the requirements that came with his decision to do so.

Several record labels seemed interested in Micah's talent, but I felt he was not mature or disciplined enough to pursue that route. I needed to make sure that Micah stayed on track with the people that had his best interest. My sole focus was Micah and getting him on track academically, along with managing his ADHD.

I continuously worked with Micah's doctor to ensure that Micah was receiving the proper medicine and follow-ups. I knew that as Micah grew older, we would have to adjust his dosages. Naturally, as a child's weight increases the medication dosage may need to be increased as well. Micah was given a small increase in dosage bits at a time. I also enrolled him in a different homeschool program. Initially, he did much better, but this could be attributed to an increase in his medication and being the new student in the school.

During his second year in the homeschool program, Micah was just non-compliant refusing to follow the rules. I was frustrated and needed support. The mentors in Micah's life were supportive. Our church members showed support, along with his uncles, Ertis and Drel. With all of the support that was in place, nothing seemed to help with improving Micah's behavior. He was non-compliant at home and school. I was in a place of questioning myself as a parent. My health was failing drastically. I did not have the energy I needed to get Micah back on track. I did not want my child to be a negative statistic. How could I not be able to help my child, yet I was skilled in the field to make a change in the lives of kids as a social worker? I also had to admit that I was putting my health on hold to focus on Micah.

We took a break from music, acting, performing, basketball, and touring. We took a break from everything. We needed to step back and regroup. I also needed Micah to understand everything he did and accomplished were earned privileges for someone his age. I also needed Micah to meet me half-way. I literally took Micah off the entertainment grid in order to save him and our relationship. As a mom, I felt disappointed and somewhat of a failure. I felt as though I failed my son and I needed help before it was too late! Deep down I knew God was preparing both Micah and me for the future and I had to trust in Him and in the process.

## <u>REFLECTION MOMENTS</u>

1. Have you connected with a mentor on behalf of your child?  If so, how have they been able to assist you with your child?

_____

_____

_____

_____

_____

2. Does your child have goals that seem impossible to achieve?  How do you encourage your child to still achieve those goals no matter how impossible they seem?

_____

_____

_____

_____

_____

3. Have you developed a schedule or routine for your child?  If so, what structure have you put into place and why?

_____

_____

_____

_____

4. Does your child have a peer group?  If so, what influence does that group have your child?

_____

_____

_____

_____

5. What is one privilege or activity that you have not allowed your child to participate in?  And why?

_____

_____

_____

_____

# NOTES

# HIGH SCHOOL YEARS

## The Storm Before the Calm

When you feel as if your back is against a wall, the natural reaction is to retreat and pray that the storm will pass. Sometimes as parents, we need to walk into the storm and pray for the strength and resources that are needed until the storm passes. It got to a point when I knew that Micah needed to have an additional outlet to make the progress that was necessary. I reached out to a psychologist that I made an acquaintance with when we initially moved to Atlanta. Within our initial conversation, I expressed my struggles with Micah. Without hesitation, I was offered to have Micah seen as a patient. I was at peace knowing that I was taking the necessary steps to see the light at the end of the tunnel. Micah, on the other hand, needed to be convinced. He was totally against therapy and felt as if he had everything under control. It was in his mindset that people just didn't "understand" him. Micah was still attending boot camp, at the time, so I had the extra help of his mentor, Domonique, to shed some light on the benefits of therapy as well. Micah reluctantly agreed to go, still believing that it wouldn't help him.

During the first few sessions, Micah remained mute in protest. He didn't react. Nor did he engage. The psychologist did all that he could to get Micah to open up and build a rapport, but Micah held up with his silent protest. I made it a point to not remain in the sessions to see if that would help with the trust building process, but that didn't make a difference either. After four sessions, Micah began to warm up. It was as if something clicked and was deemed worthy enough for Micah to start having small talk. I knew I had to trust the process and that Micah was not going to improve overnight. For whatever reason, Micah behavior at home and school continued to spiral out of control. He was taking things without permission, nonresponsive to my directives, refusing to complete school work, being untruthful. The list goes on. Micah also started to eat the lunch that I prepared in advance for me to take to work. He not only ate the lunch but would put everything back in my lunch bag as if nothing was touched. It got to a point where I started to question myself as a mother every single day. Micah was acting out in extreme ways, and it was sometimes a lot to take in.

One afternoon, as I was driving to pick up Micah from his homeschool program, I received a call from the homeschool administrator. I knew this call was important because I normally didn't receive calls from the school. The homeschool administrator began to run down a list of things that Micah was doing and continued to do. Like me, the school staff was hopeful that things would change with Micah, but that wasn't the case. What prompted the call was a recent incident where Micah showed all forms of disrespect and the decision was made to not allow him back into the homeschool program. At that moment, I knew that I couldn't fight on Micah's behalf because of where things have gotten to. I knew that everyone that was involved in Micah's life was doing their best to help him exceed, but it was Micah who was not holding up his end of the bargain.

When I got to the school to pick up Micah, I didn't have much to say to him. I was going through so many emotions. I was trying to figure out what to do with Micah since, even, homeschooling wasn't going to be an option. If it wasn't' working with this program, I knew things wouldn't work with another program. To add on top of that, I wasn't doing well health wise and needed to have major surgery in the next few months. Was he exhibiting these behaviors, because I was unable to follow through on my discipline of him? I reached out to Micah's mentors and doctors. I didn't know what to do, and I was becoming desperate. I was fed up, but I did not want to do or say anything to Micah that I would later regret. I kept asking myself how did Micah and I get to this point?

After everything that was taking place, I made the decision for Micah to attend a local public high school. Micah, of course, did not agree with my decision, but where else was he supposed to go to school? He knew that most of his bridges were burned and a schooling decision needed to be made. I enrolled Micah in Duluth High School and prayed for the best. I was doing my best in placing Micah in one of the best schools in the state of Georgia and in the country. My prayer was that things would eventually get better than what they have been.

As I transitioned Micah into a new school, I was also preparing for surgery. The last thing that I wanted to deal with was the issues that I was facing with Micah and surgery all at the same time. I couldn't put the surgery off. I held out as long as I could, but this was a non-negotiable topic with my doctors. I had to depend on Micah's mentors, heavily, during this time. My mother came to Atlanta to help out and to give me assistance following my surgery. I was limited in some things and needed the extra help staying on top of things with Micah. I trusted Micah's mentors and prayed that Micah would eventually make a turn for the best and not for the worse.

As I was recovering from surgery, Micah was also going through a transition. I went to get Micah, from his mentor's house, to find him in a changed state of mind. He was emotional when I arrived, and by the time he made it to the car, he began to cry. He apologized for everything that he was doing and acknowledged that he loved me – knowing that I truly loved him and wanted the best for him. He then began to speak about an intervention situation that he encountered in the past with his mentor, Domonique. From what I was told, Micah was introduced to some young men who acted out in more ways than one. Now that they were older, they regretted their past behaviors. They knew that if it weren't for their mothers, life would have been different from what they currently knew of. Their mothers warned them about certain life scenarios, and they didn't take heed to all things that they were told.  As we had this conversation, I could see that Micah wanted to change.  I wanted to believe he would change, but so much damage had been done.

## The Heart of the Matter

As time passed, Micah's behavior and habits started to improve. Micah and his psychologist were making progress and developing goals for Micah to achieve. Micah and I continued to have our mini struggles. Micah still felt that there wasn't a need to complete his homework nor complete his in-class assignments. I felt as if I lived at the school, due to the constant meetings that I was having with Micah's teachers. I knew there was still something going on. I just didn't know what the issue was.

One day during a therapy session, Micah's psychologist spoke to him about being adopted. I was honest with Micah about how he came into the world and into my life. I gave him the details that were appropriate, and I did so because I felt it was important for him to know about some things in his life. Micah expressed how he was sometimes angry because his biological family gave him up for adoption and kept his sibling. He was trying to grasp the fact as to why he was the child that they did not keep and his sister was the sibling they decided to keep. His psychologist then flipped the scenario and explained to Micah that as he was angry about being adopted, his sibling may be in a situation where life isn't going so well and wished that their situation was way different. It was as if a light bulb went on in Micah's head in more than one way. He realized that his life was still valuable, even after being adopted. He also learned that he truly could trust and open up to his psychologist to discuss certain issues.

My health was improving since I had my previous surgery. I was ready to get my son back on track one hundred percent. I had to reclaim my role as a disciplinary figure and let Micah know that I truly meant business. I was serious enough to draft up a contract between Micah and myself. The contract was straight to the point.

> *I, Micah Brown, agree to follow all rules at home and at school. If I decide to not follow the rules, I will accept the consequences of not being able to sleep in a comfortable bed and any other consequences that are deemed necessary.*

It was that simple. If Micah chose not to keep up with his end of the bargain, I would still feed him and allow him to take a shower, but he was not allowed to sleep in a comfortable bed. I would have thought that Micah would take this seriously. What kid does not want to sleep in a comfortable bed? Obviously, Micah thought I was initially joking after we signed this contract. He thought I was bluffing and tried to call my bluff. Micah began to realize quickly that I was not playing around. There were times that I made him sleep in the car, but he then found that to be cool. Micah no longer saw it as a punishment, so I knew I had to up the ante.

Early one Sunday morning, I dropped Micah off twenty miles from the house and told him if he truly wanted to get home, he would have to walk back. I told him he would have more than a good amount of time to think about how he was going to change his behavior and how he would handle things going forward. It took him almost eight hours to get home, but he made it back safely. When Micah arrived, he had a large smirk on his face. I couldn't believe it! I then sent him back out, to go to the store, to purchase cleaning supplies to clean his room. I would not let him in the house unless he returned with cleaning supplies. I told him that this was my house and he would not be living here if he felt the need not to follow any rules. I was trying to figure out how was Micah comfortable in this situation, and I was uncomfortable. His psychologist, my brothers, and mentors all echoed the same sentiments as we evaluated Micah's current state. They all said that Micah would not change his behavior until I made it totally uncomfortable for him. Well, he began to realize that I was not letting up on him and he became uncomfortable. Immediately, his grades began to improve, and his respect towards me changed as well. He finally got the memo that I meant business. As much as it hurt me, as a mother, to do what I did to Micah, I knew it needed to happen to save my son.

## Why Not?

Micah began to blossom and turned a new leaf during his sophomore year.  He was making friends.  He was involved in multiple community initiatives locally and nationally.  Micah was auditioning for voice over jobs and performing at events.  He was also a member of NAACP ACTSO group and volunteering.  Micah became motivated in working with other youth his age.  He was so motivated and influential that he was coordinating a monthly open mic event called *First Word* with one of his mentors, Christopher.

Micah was beginning to see the importance of giving it his all.  He was determined to show me that he wanted to do what was right in life.  Micah took online classes in the evening and the summer, all while still attending school throughout the regular school year.  His teachers saw what he was doing and wanted him to push the bar at school.  Micah's teacher eventually approached me about him taking AP English and AP Spanish.  I was totally against it mainly because I knew what Micah and I have previously gone through.  It took us a while to get us to the place where we were, and I was fearful that it would jeopardize his current progress.  Micah's teacher still pushed the issue.  Apparently, the sentiment was that Micah was not being challenged academically and felt that Micah should take a stab at AP classes.  I spoke to Micah about my concerns, and he became upset. He felt that I didn't believe in him and his ability to accomplish the proposed challenged. I had to catch myself, based on Micah's initial reaction. How dare he say that I didn't believe in him! Did he temporarily forget that I've always believed in him? I gathered my thoughts before responding to Micah. I explained to him that it wasn't the fact that I didn't believe in him. I was basing my decision on past experiences and his predictable patterns. Micah was still upset with me, even after I explained my reasons with factual truth.

He eventually spoke to one of his mentors, at church, about my unwillingness to allow him to take AP classes. His mentor asked me to clarify my reasons, and I was glad to do so. If Micah committed to taking AP classes, I would be the one taking the classes and not Micah. I would be the one having to stay on top of Micah to ensure that he completed the assignments. I would be the one continuously in contact with teachers about Micah's progress. It was a nightmare waiting to happen, and I was not willing to live through it. His mentor understood my concerns. We ultimately came to a compromise. The compromise was that Micah would enroll for honor classes and not AP classes for the upcoming school year. It wasn't what Micah wanted initially, but he knew honor classes was better than nothing. As I signed the papers and handed them to Micah, he smiled. I guess he felt that he accomplished getting his point across. That may be fine in his world, but I knew that I could not agree with him enrolling in AP classes knowing what we had been going through.

## Finishing the Race

I was hoping Micah's junior year would be better than the past two years that we experienced. Over the summer, Micah continued to earn the privilege to participate in NAACP ACT-SO competition. Since Micah became a member, he won the regional competitions and made his way to the national competitions. He traveled to Los Angles, Houston, and Orlando. Micah's talent was unquestionably real, and many wondered why he was not auditioning and appearing on television. As a mother, I knew I did not want him to live to the standards and expectations of other people – including myself to some degree. I wanted Micah to live up to his abilities in all areas of his life. I knew that he needed to follow his heart and I did not believe that acting was in his heart at the moment. Micah had other things at the top of his list: his friends and going to school to have fun. I didn't want to deprive him of those experiences. By the time he was sixteen, Micah already had his fair share of putting in hours towards acting, performing, etc. I wanted him to take the driver seat and have some say so – whether I agreed with his choices or not.

Micah was able to have a typical high school experience, but he was extremely busy. He had friends over at the house regularly. He attended football and basketball games and homecoming and prom. Micah even tried out for the cross-country team. He still did all of this while hosting open mics, working on new music, in the broadcasting club at school, being active in the church, serving on the Board for the Stewart Foundation, and the list goes on. Micah also worked a part-time job at Sonics. He was a regular kid, and he deserved to be one at this point of his life.

Micah's hard work with his online classes paid off in a major way that neither one of us expected. One day he came home and told me he had a meeting with his school counselor. She informed him that he had enough school credits to graduate his junior year. Who would've thought that with all the struggles we went through, academically, that this boy would end up graduating a year early! Micah was beyond ecstatic when he heard this news. He didn't know what to do with himself at first. But then it hit him that he was finishing school at seventeen, and quickly being able to move on in life.

Planning for life after high school was challenging – for the both of us. Whenever I asked Micah what his plans were, he would quickly tell me that he was working on his plans. I knew not to pressure him, but he needed to know that his life wouldn't consist of lying in bed all day. To explore Micah's options, we went on a college tour. In all, we visited eight different colleges in the state of Georgia. Micah made it clear he did not want to go to college out of state. He said he wanted to be close to home. During the college courting process, Micah's actions were not lining up with his words. He did not complete any college applications and never spoke on where he wanted to go. Micah just walked around like he had no care in the world. I did not want Micah to think he did not have other options, but he was the one who communicated he wanted to go to college after graduating. I could only go by what he said, but his actions were speaking louder than his words. Micah eventually opted to go to a two-year college. It wasn't what we originally discussed, but I knew he had to come to that decision on his own. Now, all we needed to do was focus getting through the rest of the year.

As graduation day approached, Micah and I were both excited. My son that was doomed from the day he was born was graduating a year early, and that was something to be more than grateful for. As life would have its way, I became very sick the week before Micah's graduation date. It was so severe that I needed emergency surgery and was going to be hospitalized. How could this be happening! This was supposed to be a week of celebrations and fun. Not be ending up in the hospital during one of the most important times of Micah's life.

My mother came to Atlanta, earlier than expected, to assist with things as I prepped for surgery. I was more concerned for Micah than I was for myself. He was in the middle of his finals and preparing to graduate, but there was nothing that I could do at this point. I required surgery, and I had to hope for the best.

Micah stepped up tremendously – beyond my expectations to be honest. Micah showed much responsibility during the time that it mattered most. He got up and off to school on time each day on his own. Micah completed all his assignments and studied to pass all his finals. He did his chores. Micah was the young man I knew he could become.

Finally, it was graduation day! I was still recovering from surgery but obtained clearance to participate in one of the most unforgettable days in both of our lives. Joined by close friends, Micah's mentors and our family, I watched Micah walk across the stage to receive his diploma. It was as if time stood still long enough for me to take in that very moment – a moment that I still cherish to this very day. Micah achieved something that most, born in the same circumstances, do not achieve. He never required special education services throughout his entire schooling. Micah was never academically slower than other students his age, which was evident by his graduating his junior year. Micah achieved greatness his way, and that's all that mattered.

## REFLECTION MOMENTS

1. How do you handle frustration that is caused by your child?

_____

_____

_____

_____

_____

2. Who do you turn to for support after you have tried everything you know of to assist your child?

_____

_____

_____

_____

_____

3. What discipline techniques do you find most difficult even though you know it is necessary for your child to change behavior?

_____

_____

_____

_____

_____

_____

4. How do you develop standards and goals for your child?

_____

_____

_____

_____

_____

# NOTES

# WHAT'S NEXT?!

## I Choose College…I Think

Have you planned out your child's life and to your naïve surprise things didn't go the way you expected?  After Micah graduated from high school, I just knew that he was well on his way to a successful college career.  I mean, I knew that he would have some learning curves with keeping up with the demands and expectations of college, but I was hopeful.  Well…That wasn't the case.  Micah enrolled in a two-year college, started his classes, and held on to old habits.  He didn't do the required work, nor did he turn in the requested assignments.  Micah was eligible for assistance and benefits, based on his disability, but he refused to take advantage of what was being offered.  Ultimately, he had to leave the school.

Over time, it seemed as if Micah was just going through the motions.  He continued with his usual things.  He was also still going to his therapy sessions, but that's all it seemed to be.  Micah was just existing.  Micah and I eventually had a heart to heart.  Within that conversation, Micah honestly told me that he did not want to attend college.  He only enrolled because he thought that's what I wanted him to do and that it would make me happy.  Micah then went on to express that he wanted to dedicate his time to make music again.  It was something that was always a part of him, and he didn't want to neglect it.  Even with what he was telling me, within this very conversation, I was irate.  I felt that all of this could have truly been avoided. I was upset because I asked Micah, multiple times if he was sure that college was the way to go. "Yes!" was always his answer. If I would've known the truth upfront, so much time and money wouldn't have been wasted. I understood, to a degree where Micah was coming from, but I couldn't co-sign on how he handled things. Nor could I agree with him just making music. I told him he needed to get involved in some education program or get a job. I was not going to allow him to live in my house just to pursue music. Don't get me wrong. I have always supported Micah's dream, but I also always taught him how to be responsible. Living in my house to just make music wouldn't be responsible. It would be a complete luxury.

Micah obviously knew that I was not playing around with him after that discussion. He applied to some jobs and finally got hired at Aldi. Micah was making good money as a teenager, but that also became a distraction. All Micah did was work! Many times, he was working sixteen-hour days and not focusing on his music. I quickly reminded Micah of what he said he wanted out of life. I asked if he was content with just working at Aldi and making a career out of it. I wasn't discouraging Micah from the accomplishments that he achieved while working, but I also did not want him to forget where his heart was. His heart was in his music. Micah openly admitted that he wanted more in life, he just didn't know how to get back on track.

Now that Micah recognized where he was in life, we were back at square one to decide what he wanted to do in life. I asked Micah the million-dollar question. "What do you want to do with your life?" Micah confidently responded that he wanted to become a fireman. It took everything within me to tell my child that he could not be a fireman. He was diagnosed as severe asthmatic and with ADHD. How in the world could this boy become a fireman?! Of course, I didn't' say what I was thinking. I just went along with Micah's idea of him wanting to be a fireman. He quit his job at Aldi and registered in an EMT program at a local college. Even as skeptical as I was, I still needed to show my support.

Micah became motivated again. He kept his grades up within the EMT program. He started to write music again. Additionally, Micah began to audition for movies. He was doing what he wanted to do, and I could see that based on his motivation. One day, Micah got the news that due to his health, it would be difficult for him to pass the required physical exams that were issued to become a fireman. He accepted the information from the medical professional, but he was very disappointed. I felt really bad for Micah. I knew that he was really hoping to accomplish this one thing and it wasn't going to happen. I did not know how to make it better for him but knew that I just needed to be there to support him through this.

## There is Always an Answer

It wasn't a secret about Micah's talents when it came to technology. Although he ventured into a lot of areas, in life, Micah was always great with computers and technology. One day, one of Micah's mentors asked him why wasn't he working with computers. Micah and I both knew that working in the technology field required dedication and time, but it would also give Micah the flexibility to work on the other things that he loved to do. We both began to research local programs and came across the Year Up program. Micah felt the program was too good to be true, but he applied anyway. In my research, I found out that this program required all participants to adhere to strict policies and requirements in order to remain in the program for its full duration. I wanted Micah to be successful, but I also had to remind him that I wouldn't be able to save him from most responsibilities that he took on. This was a program that Micah couldn't slack in nor act nonchalant. Micah said that he was ready to take on the challenge to pursue greatness.

Micah was accepted into the Year Up program. During the parent orientation, it was made clear that the staff knew that the participants of the program did not want to live under the "influence" of their parents. The staff stated that the participants needed to recognize what they truly wanted for their own lives. I could do nothing but agree with them. Micah, at the time, was twenty years old and he needed to figure out life without my prompting and chastising. I knew that he could achieve anything, but he needed to see that for himself.

The Year Up program was in session five days a week. There weren't any negotiations, and Micah had to be present all days for classes. There weren't any excuses for being late either. All assignments needed to be turned in early or on time. No assignments were accepted past the due date. If any of the program participants couldn't keep up with the requirements, they would be asked to leave the program. I saw a different Micah, as he participated in the Year Up program. He was waking up on time without my assistance. He reminded himself to take his daily medication. He became more proactive with preparing for things the day before his classes. Micah was doing more than what I've seen him do in the past. This is how I knew he wanted better and wanted to change. Everyone could see it in his actions. I could see it when it was time for him to handle his day to day responsibilities. Micah was performing above and beyond despite his disabilities.

I couldn't allow Micah's change to go unnoticed. I contacted one of his mentors, within the Year Up program, to thank him for the time that had been dedicated to working with Micah. I was, then, made privy to the fact that Micah's peers truly looked up to him. Although his peers were able to see Micah's flaws, they still looked up to him and sought his assistance whenever they needed help academically. I knew that Micah was finally finding his own way, but more importantly also finding himself.

## Beyond Motivated

As Micah navigated his way through the Year Up program, things began to fall into place. Our relationship was being restored day by day. Things just seemed to be different. Micah was becoming more motivated. Micah was so motivated that he wanted to release a new album for his twenty-first birthday. He wanted to make it a big event with friends and family. That meant Micah would have to be able to keep up with the demands of the program and producing a full album. It also meant that I would have to finance everything since Micah wasn't working. I had to think about what would be required on both of our parts. After thinking about things, I agreed to invest into his project – with it being the last time that I would. I told Micah that I would do this as part of his birthday wish, but going forward if he wanted to pursue music he would have to fund it himself. Micah understood my approach and agreed to my requirements.

We began the footwork that was needed to get the album produced. Micah wanted to put out a quality album, and that was going to take a qualified team. We contacted recording studios and record producers in Georgia, New York, California, and Ohio to get music for him to write his songs. There was a particular sound that Micah was looking for, so we had to be selective on who we worked with. As a result, Micah decided to go with Gamble, Buddah Munroe, and Billy Hume to record and produce his album. We had to be particular in what the marketing campaign entailed, along with what songs would eventually make it to the album. This was the biggest and most expensive album project Micah has taken on within his whole career.

Keep in mind, Micah not only had to keep up with the demands of getting an album done, but he also had to keep up with the demands of the Year Up program. Once he started working on his music, his day was occupied with school work and studio time. There was nothing else in between. Micah was finally following his heart while learning how to be successful in the technology field. I felt relieved as a parent. My son was finally finding his footing in a world that he sometimes didn't fit in with. He was gaining the acceptance of not only with his peers but also with the adults that he met. Everyone could see the heart that Micah had, not only for music but also for the everyday life issues that were paraded across the world.

As part of the Year Up program, all participants are required to complete an internship. This was a requirement that had to be completed to graduate from the program. A company called VM Ware Airwatch selected Micah for their internship program – to work as a technical support assistant. Yet again, this was something else being added to Micah's plate to keep up with along with everything else he was accomplishing. The day before Micah was to begin his internship, he told me he was feeling an excruciating pain in his big toe. My immediate reaction was to take him to the urgent care, but Micah refused. He was quite adamant about not being stuck in a hospital overnight because he wanted to be well rested and prepared for his internship. I pleaded that he go to the hospital, in fear that something could really be wrong, but Micah insisted not to. He agreed to go after he completed his first day as an intern if the pain did subside. As Micah would have it, he went to his first day of his internship with a throbbing toe. I later took him to the urgent care, to find out that Micah had an ingrown toenail. The doctor prescribed some medicine for Micah's toe, which alleviated the pain and cured the condition. All along, while Micah was administering the medicine, he made it a point to remind me that I was worrying over nothing. Yes, I could only worry as a mother, but I continued to see the dedication that Micah had for all that needed to be accomplished. We could've gone to the urgent care when I suggested, but I also knew that I needed to allow Micah to make certain decisions – regardless of the outcome.

As we planned Micah's twenty-first birthday celebration and album release party, he proactively spread the word to family and friends. He wanted everyone close to him to celebrate his success and the new chapters of his life. Micah recorded forty songs in preparation for his album. Yes, I said forty. Micah was on a mission to making this not just an album of music, but an album that reflected him as the man that he was becoming. I believe Micah felt he had to prove something to everyone.

Especially to those that commented on him as an artist – being better than those in today's mainstream industry. Many people questioned why Micah's music wasn't on television, in movies, or on the radio. They were boggled by the fact that Micah wasn't signed to a major record label. I know those questions haunted Micah in some ways and made him feel as if he should be doing more when it came to his music. In his moments of frustration, I could only remind Micah that God's plan for him isn't what the world thought of him.

## Twenty-One and Legal

Micah's birthday arrived, and I had to accept the fact that my son was twenty-one. He wasn't the scrawny little kid that most knew by the name of "Lil' Dude." He was twenty-one and legal.

His party was on the actual day of his birthday, which made the day even more special for him. Micah put a lot of work into the album and the planning of his party. Some family traveled to Atlanta to celebrate with him. People from the music industry, friends from high school, friends from Year Up, mentors, and fans were also in attendance. Micah secured sponsorships from over ten companies to sponsor the event. When Micah performed, it was evident that he was in his element. It was clear and evident that Micah did not have a care in the world! As a mother, I was proud. Micah accomplished so much to make this day happen, and I just went along for the ride. After it was all said and done, Micah told me that this birthday was one of the best birthdays that he has ever had.

After Micah's party, I saw that he was striving to prove himself even more to be a man. Micah was taking more of an initiative towards his future. He knew he was graduating in a few months, so he updated his resume. He, independently, applied to local universities and other jobs in order to have something lined up after graduation. Micah attended countless interviews and studied many companies of interest. As his graduation from

Year Up approached, Micah was offered a job. Micah was not only becoming a man, he was truly taking control of his life.

The day of graduation, Micah was rushing me out of the house because he didn't want to be late for the ceremony. I had to step back and take in this moment. Before, I was the one getting onto Micah about managing his time. Now, here he was making it a point to be on time for another special moment in his life. It was so much to take in, especially as I looked back over the past few years and reflected on what we've been through. As Micah walked across the stage to receive his certificate, I knew he was walking into a new chapter of his life, and I was proud of him. It was also a moment where I reflected on God's promise to me. I let His words simmer in my heart, and I truly believed, at that moment, that Micah will be used to touch millions.

At the ceremony, it appeared that every Year Up instructor knew Micah. He introduced me to everyone that he knew. He was all over the place. One of his instructors expressed her love for Micah but also had to acknowledge how she had to keep up with him and his hyperactive behavior. I could only share her sentiment because it was a song that I've heard from many before her. If I had a penny for every time someone expressed their "love-hate" feelings for Micah's behaviors, I would really be a millionaire.

A lot became clear to me as I watched Micah accomplish another milestone. I finally understood that all children have a gift and it is up to us, as parents, to recognize those gifts. It is also up to us to put them in situations to succeed and improve the lives of others. To get Micah to the point of where he was successfully completing a demanding program, releasing another album, and applying for jobs of his choosing, was one heck of a challenge. BUT... It was a challenge that was worth it!

# REFLECTION MOMENTS

1. How can your child's "flaws/difference" be viewed as a strength to the world?

_____

_____

_____

_____

2. What moment has your child achieved something regardless of the odds that were against him/her?

_____

_____

_____

_____

3. Who do you consider your child's support team and why?

_____

_____

_____

_____

# NOTES

## **Reflections of a Role Mother**

Over the years, plenty of people have questioned me about my parenting approach relating to Micah. Random individuals have stopped me to say/ask:

"You are raising a young man that has impressive mannerisms!"

"How were you able to do all those activities with him?"

"Can I talk to you? I have a son with ADHD, and I don't know what to do anymore."

"I don't want my son to become a zombie! What worked for Micah?"

The list of statements and questions can go on for days. The point is that I always found myself in the midst of explaining my parenting experiences. I received a true revelation after Micah's graduation luncheon. My pastor at the time encouraged me to put my experiences in a book to help other mothers like myself. It was as if the light bulb went off. Not to say that I did not like the face to face interactions when others would approach me, but I looked at it as a way to reach people that I may not even meet in person. So, with that said...this is the book that God placed in my heart to write.

There is no true handbook on parenting. Especially when each child is different. You may have more than one child, but each child is different in their own God given right. As parents, we should embrace those differences. While parenting Micah, I always kept that in mind. As hard as it is to believe, I had no specific expectations of what I wanted Micah to become as a man. I knew that God has a calling on his life, but I also knew that Micah would ultimately have a say in the person that he became. I always kept *Proverbs 22:6* close to my heart. It teaches you to train up your children, in such a way that they will not forget what they were taught as they get older. I believe that you should not just train up your children with the basics, but also train them within their purpose and passions. It wasn't hard for me to realize what Micah was supposed to do when he grew up, it was just a matter of positioning him to be able to achieve it. It was critical that, as a mother, I identified the tools I wanted Micah to have as he matured throughout life and surrounded him with people who I believe possessed those tools.

As a single mother, raising a son, I knew from the beginning that I could not do it alone. I knew I needed support and encouragement for both Micah and myself. It is not easy to raise a child. It is definitely not easy to raise a child with special needs or disabilities. BUT…raising a child, should always be rewarding. I remember something that my brother, Drel, once told me. He said that I should really look at the fact that Micah not only needed me in his life. It was also a matter of me needing Micah in my life. When Drel made that statement, I honestly knew that was God's plan all along.

When Micah was young, I never would have imagined that my son will have over forty mentors. I just knew that he needed other people in his life besides me. I truly believe that is does take a village to raise a child. Micah had a village. There are so many instances where his village stepped up to assist with Micah. All of Micah's mentors impressed me immensely. I know that I could never pay them back for all things they have done for Micah. Their value and presence were priceless! I only hope that Micah would pay it forward, as I have taught him to.

One of Micah's mentors, was a deep inspiration for me while writing this book. He is a person that has dedicated his life to the youth of metropolitan Atlanta. At a difficult time, in Micah's life, he handed Micah an opportunity to become the man I knew he could be. He followed up, checked in with Micah, and showed Micah how to be a man by being a true living example. He would never know the impact that he has had on Micah's life, since coming into Micah's life at the early age of eleven. He has seen Micah's highs and lows, but through it all, he never gave up on Micah. Neither of Micah's mentors gave up. That is a testament to their characters as human beings. It's as if everyone wanted Micah to win!

Speaking of winning, as a mother, I found myself on the sideline coaching and cheering Micah on. I used the philosophy of coaching when parenting him. As a coach, I practiced and practiced. There were plenty of times when Micah would become angry at me because he wanted to just do what he wanted without any repercussions. We all know that is not the reality of the world in which we live. In life, there are always consequences for our actions. Consequences are not good or bad. They are just the result of our actions or behaviors. Micah needed to know that. I coached him in the game of life to be prepared. I knew that I could only prepare him by making certain tools and resources available to him. Some may consider my parenting technique unorthodox, but I knew what it would take to save my child from his own destruction and the status quo of this world. Micah was already born with strikes against him. I didn't want him to be *limited in life* because of the strikes that were counted against him. When Micah wasn't following the game plan, he was benched. It was just that plain and simple.

One thing that I taught Micah, as a child and young adult, was to be able to utilize the tools and resources that were made accessible to him. Whether if it is the tools to be able to make his own decisions or the resources of being able to call on a mentor, I wanted Micah to know that he plays a part in his own life. As you can see within this book, I supported Micah in many of his decisions - regardless if I believed it was not the right decision. I did not support him if I felt his decision would cause severe harm to him or someone else - physically and/or emotionally. If I did not support Micah in a decision, I would make it a point to explain why and give other suggestions.

I believe each of us is entitled to live our lives under our terms regardless of our disabilities or life's circumstances. Everyone should be allowed to take risks. That is a normal part of life. I taught Micah to learn from his failures as well as to learn from his success. There should always be a balance. When Micah was younger, he did not understand this concept much. I knew as he got older it would make more sense to him.

I always taught Micah to never be afraid to ask for what he want or need, especially if he don't have it at the time. We must put our pride to the side to go out and conquer the world. Rejection is natural. I know that, as parents, we will do anything and everything to shield our children from the things that may hurt them. Whether, if we try to shield them from rejection or the "realities" of life, we interfere with their true development when we play a god in our children's lives. They have to experience certain events in order for them to learn a lesson and become stronger in life.

I can recall a time when Micah and I were at a computer store to purchase equipment for his recording studio. When it was time to check out, I asked the cashier if I could receive a discount on the current purchase. The cashier kindly told me that she was not authorized to give me a discount. In return, I asked who had the authority to grant the discount. The cashier stated that her manager would be the one to authorize such transaction. While this transaction of words took place, Micah was becoming uneasy with what was going on. He looked at me as if I was embarrassing him and making a big issue out of nothing. Despite his silent disapproval, I pressed on. As the manager approached, I asked if I could have a discount on the current purchase. The manager was taken aback and asked if there was anything wrong. I unquestionably told her that there wasn't anything wrong. I then went on to say that all of the products that I purchase from this store is always of good quality and the customer service is always more than exceptional. Still confused, the manager asked for a reason for me wanting a discount. I confidently told the manager that I am a loyal customer and I spend more than enough money in the store. For that reason, alone, I believed that I deserved some type of discount. The manager tilted her head to think for a moment. She then verified my account and previous purchases. The next thing I know, the manager told the cashier to authorize a twenty percent discount on my current purchase. I thanked the manager and the cashier while prompting Micah with a look to do the same. As the manager walked away, the cashier exclaimed that she never saw the manager approve such a request in her history of working at the store. After this learning moment, for Micah, I explained to him that I am not afraid to ask for what I need or want. I told him to think about what would have been the worst thing that could happen. He admittedly told me that the manager could've just declined the request. He now understood that it truly never really hurts to ask. Even if the request were declined, it wouldn't have been the end of the world. I still would've purchased the items. I just wanted Micah to see what it looks like to self-advocate for something that you need or want.

Life is a process and, as parents, we should allow the space for our children to grow and learn. Let them take risks! Let them make mistakes! Let them have fun! Let them plan their future with your guidance! It's their future, not ours. Whether we agree with their decisions or not, we have to respect that ultimately it is their decision. Never compare your child to someone else. Only see your child as an individual. It's okay to encourage a child to outdo themselves. Encourage them to lift the ceiling, until they reach the top. Please do know that each child's ceiling is different. Know your child and what makes them want to keep going. All children have the capacity to be winners. All children are winners if, and only if, we give them the proper tools and opportunities to win!

We must develop a "different mindset" on how and why we parent our children the way we do. We all can be the "role mother" our children need win in the game of life. We must be able to confidently tell our children that the sky is the limit, as we encourage them to reach for the sky. Micah Brown is living proof!

"To know Micah is to love him." – William "Uncas" Walker (Micah's Mentor)

To all the men that stepped up and played a critical role in Micah's life (his village), I am thankful and grateful for all the hours of your time that you gave my son, Micah.

Windale (godfather), Ertis (uncle), Drel (uncle), Clarence (uncle), Derrick (cousin), Ross "Spiderman" (cousin), Marcellus, Christopher "Cocktails", Abyss, Tommy "Gamble", Dave Tolliver, Hank Stewart, Hakim Green, Billy Hume, Glenn Brooks, Speech, Domonique, Buddah, George "Gee", Victor Burnett, Ward, Job, Legend, Rodney L., Rodney S., Dave S., Mr. Gentry, Viva Fidel, Shady Dude, Darryl S., Darrell E., Kevin D., DJ Strong, Sir Rod, Brandon M., Deshaun, Monyea, Carlos, Mike, Pohhla, Kwebna, DJ Kutt, Brian, Duane "Spyda", Llew H., Dewayne, Kevin S., Henderson "Mr. 23", Capp, Reggie, and Dre'.

Although Micah never had an earthly father, he's had many men who have been life-long mentors, father figures, role models, surrogate uncles, big brothers and lastly, his friend... Too many to name everyone!

# Your Next Steps

☐ **Visit www.MsTelah.com to take the Role Mother Assessment.**
After you complete the assessment, you will receive an e-mail to schedule your free assessment

☐ **Register for a MATH session with MsTelah.**
Visit www.MsTelah.com for more information.

☐ **Review your answers from the Reflection Moments.**
Note the following:
- ✓ Your take-a-ways.
- ✓ Things you need help with overall.
- ✓ Things you would like to overall change.

☐ **Register for a MsTelah event in your local area.**
Visit www.MsTelah.com to view the tour schedule. If MsTelah isn't scheduled to come to a city near you, submit a request!

☐ **Text @MsTelah to 81010 to receive real time updates and information.**
You must include the @ symbol when sending your initial text.

☐ **Visit Amazon and write a review about this book.**
We love to receive feedback on everything! Please write an honest review on Amazon.

☐ **Follow MsTelah on social media @MsTelah.**
Be sure to send MsTelah a message to let her know that you read this book and how it helped you!

www.ingramcontent.com/pod-product-compliance
Lightning Source LLC
Chambersburg PA
CBHW081150090426
42736CB00017B/3262